My oldest will turn eleven this year. So basically, I've been tired for a decade. Stacey Thacker is the voice in my head telling me I'm going to be okay. This book is your permission slip to stop feeling like you have to be all things to all people all the time.

Lisa-Jo Baker, author of *Surprised by Motherhood* and community manager for (in)courage

This book came to me at a vulnerable time in my life when I couldn't have felt less amazing. After reading Stacey's gentle yet powerful words, I knew a welcomed, hope-filled revival in my spirit. Without a doubt, *Fresh Out of Amazing* is the meeting place where your tired, worn-out heart finds God's gifts of tender mercy and renewed strength.

Kristen Strong, author of *Girl Meets Change*

Stacey's words sweep me off my feet and put me on my knees in worship to the One we all long to know and love. With the voice of a tender mentor, the heart of a kindred-spirited friend, and the wisdom of a seasoned disciple of Christ, Stacey wins my heart. Her inviting words, rich biblical teaching, and a wealth of practical insight will guide you from the land of lies and lack to a wide and spacious place filled with hope, anchored in Truth.

Francie Winslow, speaker and writer

Stacey is a born encourager. For years, I've watched God use her words of wisdom to bring clarity and courage to women, propelling us toward the everyday purposes and dreams God has for us. Through *Fresh Out of Amazing*, you'll be influenced to enjoy and worship God—even through the driest and darkest places of your life.

Katie Orr, author of the FOCUSed15 Bible study

In *Fresh Out of Amazing*, Stacey lets us know that on those many days when we just have nothing left, we are not alone. But she doesn't leave us with just having a friend who understands. With the power of God's Word, she takes us by the hand and s

exactly what we need to not just ke

In the midst of my own world of burdened and busy, I settle my jaded self in the pages of this book. Stacey Thacker has understood me. She has heard me, without me saying a word. *Fresh Out of Amazing* gives me the permission to exhale over the frailties of my life I often try to avoid. I am moved, hopeful, and grateful.

Lisa Whittle, author of *{w}hole* and *I Want God*

Stacey is the friend you call when you are at the end of yourself and you need someone to speak equal parts truth and grace over you. Within these pages you will find a kind companion who knows the heartache life can bring. Stacey is a generous guide who uses Scripture and story to point us back to the God who captures our tears and draws us near.

Teri Lynne Underwood, founder of *Prayers for Girls*

No matter what season of life you find yourself in, there's always a need to feel like someone understands you. Stacey Thacker is that person, and in *Fresh Out of Amazing*, you will find that "I've been there too" encouragement.

Clare Smith, writer/speaker/blogger at claresmith.me

Fresh Out of Amazing is a soul-filling, heart-reviving invitation to open your heart to God's life-changing work. These Scripture-soaked words present the power of God's grace and the gift of His hope in a way that's relevant for any woman on a journey of faith.

Elisa Pulliam, author of *Meet the New You*

I could tell you Stacey Thacker is a great writer, because she is. I could tell you she's a great mother, because she is that too. Wife, friend, and singer extraordinaire, that's her. But the best thing about Stacey is her ability to share the deep, sometimes hard, truths in a way that leaves you loving Jesus more than when you started. In a world that says we have to be amazing to measure up, Stacey points to grace.

Brooke McGlothlin, coauthor of *Hope for the Weary Mom*

This book feels like the truest kind of friendship shared over a cup of coffee with your shoes kicked off. Stacey is authentic, insightful, and devoted to helping women discover how to return to the One who is always amazing when we're fresh out.

Crystal Stine, author of *Creative Basics*

STACEY THACKER

Fresh Out of Amazing

HARVEST HOUSE PUBLISHERS
EUGENE, OREGON

Cover by Brian Bokel Design

Published in association with the Books & Such Management, 52 Mission Circle, Suite 122, PMB 170, Santa Rosa, CA 95409-5370, www.booksandsuch.com.

FRESH OUT OF AMAZING

Copyright © 2016 Stacey Thacker
Published by Harvest House Publishers
Eugene, Oregon 97402
www.harvesthousepublishers.com

ISBN 978-0-7369-6734-1 (pbk.)
ISBN 978-0-7369-6735-8 (eBook)

Printed in the United States of America

16 17 18 19 20 21 22 23 24 / VP-CD / 10 9 8 7 6 5 4 3 2 1

For Mike
You were right, of course, about the writing thing.

Acknowledgments

If God has called you to something, you will need friends to help you be brave.

SHAUNA NIEQUIST

With gratitude for those who helped me be brave:

Mike: Being married to a fresh-out-of-amazing girl is not easy. Thank you for your grace every day. I wouldn't be standing here in this place without your support and encouragement. Love you. Always.

My girls: I will always respond with a smile when others say, "Are all these girls yours?" I have the best job in the world as your mom. Thanks for being endlessly patient with your writer mom. Love you so much!

Angie Elkins, Emily Blackwell, Teri Lynne Underwood, Tanya Cramer, Lainie Thomas, Krystal Nowak, Robin Langford, Gretchen Scoleri, Unchong Berkey, and Michal Lynn Tweedie: Your help on this manuscript was irreplaceable. Sending timid words to sweet friends who are more like sisters is so much easier. Praying I can do the same for you. Also, I owe you coffee.

Voxer Girls (Kat Lee, Amy Lynn Andrews, Katie Orr, Lara Williams, Chrystal Hurst, Francie Winslow, Liz Griffin, and Heather MacFadyen): You are the best kind of gift. You are strong, Jesus-loving, purposeful women of faith who challenge and encourage me to follow hard after Him. Grateful for each and every one of you!

Brooke: This book has hovered in the background of *Hope* for the past few years. Thank you for your encouragement to write these words and for your support. I missed writing *with* you, friend.

Sara Hagerty: It means more to me than you will ever know to have your words in this book. Thank you for not only saying yes, but praying first. Simply grateful, sweet friend.

Janet Grant and the Books & Such Agency: I am so grateful for our timely meeting at Allume. You were the first to tell me to write this book. God knew what I needed in an agent and your wisdom has been invaluable. Thank you for always steering me right and caring with all of your heart!

Kathleen Kerr: You are golden. Thank you for pushing me to write the book that fresh-out-of-amazing readers need. I can't wait to hug your neck and buy you a white mocha.

Mom: Thank you for not losing your song in the valley of bitterness and grief. You are still singing and I am so proud to be your daughter!

Dad: Missing you still. Comforted by this thought: "Better is one day in your courts than a thousand elsewhere" (Psalm 84:10 NIV). I know you are having the best day ever. See you soon.

Contents

Foreword by Sara Hagerty

I managed to crumple into a heap on my bed while holding the babe. I was still a mother, even in this melted state. I finally released the kind of tears you cry when a dozen times previous they've been stifled.

These weren't just today's sobs.

The questions I'd been evading for weeks, perhaps even months, fell into my mind like bombs being dropped by planes overhead, strafing across my otherwise rational thinking.

Who was I to think I could live my life well—this life right in front of me—and with any sense of joy?

At what point did I move from having a good handle on my priorities to just surviving my days?

Have I just messed this all up? What is wrong with me that I'm here, now, unable to hold it together?

I clamped my eyes shut, over the tears, as if I could somehow close the door on all the questions, the insecurity, the creeping sense of failure, and go on to make a fantastic gourmet dinner in a spotless kitchen. As if I could even press pause on the swirling around me for long enough to pray, or even form a sentence or grab a tissue.

They were shut for five seconds before the baby cried, joining me in my meltdown and reminding me that I didn't have the luxury of time to gain perspective on this internal rift. And then a knock at the door and I heard a squabble down the hall, between which there was a lineup of blocks in primary colors scattered across my hallway.

How did I get here? And what do I do now?

The questions and tears kept coming, no longer minding the children's interruptions, no longer minding that I considered myself to be too old to be undone like this. I couldn't ignore the internal noise within my head and my heart anymore, telling me I was losing in this season of life.

I needed a brush with God, right there—right in the middle of yesterday's laundry and today's unmet expectations and the baby's swollen gums.

We've held onto the same white matelassé bedcover for ten years—and it's still white, not dulled or gray. Through wall color changes and new pillowcases and switched-out duvet covers and house moves, that comforter has steadily fielded one of these meltdowns of mine (at least) per year.

Once a year, or after each time we've added a child to our family or said yes to a new aspect of God's call on our life, I have one. I can pass off this meltdown as merely being the result of this new addition to our family or this added element in our lives. But in truth the change is only serving as the catalyst to unearth the deeper thoughts and questions of my heart—about myself and about God.

This long-resisted place, where I finally fold and foist a white flag in the air that says, "I can't do this, this way, anymore," if tended to properly, is holy. Sacred.

It's here that I get my brush with God, where His fingers press against what hurts inside me and He shows me another side of Himself, the side I've been most needing to see. Most craving. I no longer resent the once-harsh realization that I am "fresh out of amazing" if it means that this admission, finally spoken out loud or whispered in the back alley of my heart, admits me into His presence in a new way.

To admit "I am fresh out of amazing" is to find your melody in the life-anthem of every human, caught in the nexus of skin and God's accessible glory. We were made for the kind of amazing in God that the very best version of ourselves could never produce, even just for one hour of our entire lives.

Paul describes this truth of our human limitations, against the power of Him, in one statement that makes me think that coming to "fresh out of amazing" might just be the turning point in all of life: "Now to Him who is able to do exceedingly abundantly above all that we ask or think, according to the power that works in us" (Ephesians 3:20 NKJV).

And in the pages that follow this foreword, you'll find a friend saying it again—saying it with His Word as the backdrop. Saying it by way of her accessible vulnerability. Saying it as one who has traversed over and through the shock of her own limitations and into the invasively beautiful invitation of God. Saying it as one who has found Him to be more than amazing.

This book is a long conversation with a big sister who is looking you straight in the eye and inviting you to take a break from biting your fingernails and to see just how very beautiful the end of yourself might be. If you read with a hungry heart—hungry to climb right out of yourself and into a deep inhalation of a fresh perspective of Him and of you—you will not close the back cover unchanged.

Several years ago when I met Stacey in person for the first time at a conference, she slid off her shoes and sat cross-legged in my stilted hotel room, over takeout, coaching me through a fear I was facing in writing. She looked straight in my eyes, unashamedly describing her own follow-through on a nudge from Him to write, and infused me with the unique courage that comes when a human realizes their own limitations while in the hands of a big God. She preached the message of this book to me in the midst of my heart-churn, over bad pizza and wood veneer furniture.

Within these pages is a fresh message with fresh life in it from a unique and powerful voice who is, herself, fresh out of her own kind of amazing. Whether read in one sitting or while taking long sips over a longer season of life, come vulnerable. Open. Come without posturing—but instead admitting, alongside all the others standing on the shore of great possibility in God, *I need a fresh brush with God.* Come ready to look Him in the eye. Rather, come prepared to have Him look you in yours, and tenderly. Come with the anthem of ages—*I'm approaching the end of myself*—with a pen in hand, ready to scratch out those new notes. Because He's writing a tenderly beautiful song with your life—yes, that life of yours that's fresh out of amazing.

Part 1

Hello, Fresh-Out-of-Amazing Girl

I see it in your eyes as you force a kind smile and simultaneously hold back tears when I ask you how you are doing. All day long, you've felt like everything is falling apart, and you are trying to keep it all together. You are running everywhere and feeling responsible for everything. But in this moment you are tired. *You are so very tired of being the one who is strong and dependable and brave.*

I understand, my sweet friend, more than you know. In fact, I think I can safely say that we both understand the phrase *fresh out of amazing* without needing a dictionary to explain it. We feel it deep in our souls.

We have hearts full of good intentions, but we have a tendency to overestimate our own awesomeness. This mind-set worked well for us—until we walked by the mirror and caught a glimpse of the tired, worn-thin lady looking back at us. We didn't much like what we saw, so we hurried past, grabbed our coffee-on-the-go cup, and out the door we went. *Maybe she won't be there when we get back,* we thought. We hoped.

I understand your tiredness because, like you, I've been trying so hard to become a better version of myself. Only I think I lost her in the process. Or maybe I found her and didn't really like her. What do you do when you are living out the storyline of your life and you don't like the way your character is behaving?

For a long time, I didn't like my character—and I didn't know how to fix her. So I ignored Miss Fresh-Out-of-Amazing because no one else seemed to notice. After all, people usually don't linger long enough to look intently. They accept "fine" as the answer to "How are you doing?" and move along their merry way.

Hiding was the easy part. And I did it pretty well.

Then one day everything began to change. I found myself desperately wanting to quit my job, and I went so far as to write my resignation letter. That course of action sounds perfectly respectable…except the job I really wanted to quit wasn't at a fancy office that accepts resignations on the third Tuesday of the month. It was the one job I had always known I wanted: being a mom. But where does a mom go when she wants to resign?

You see the problem, don't you?

I'm guessing you feel the same way. I didn't really want to resign. I just wanted to escape needing to be amazing and finding myself fresh out. But can I tell you something I've learned recently? Fresh out of amazing keeps bubbling up to the top because it has deep roots in my life. Does it for you too?

That idea of deep roots reminds me of the movie *Groundhog Day*. Bill Murray plays a weatherman stuck in a time loop. Every day he wakes up and discovers it is still Groundhog Day. His version of living the same day over and over again is slightly funnier than the one I'm playing out. The struggle is real. I'm practically a professional at feeling this way. In some ways I would tell you it is simply what I do to keep going. It is how I get things done. Or, lately, why I'm not getting anything done.

Are you nodding your head in agreement? Finally, somebody has pulled back the curtain and revealed that the wizard behind the whole operation is really just a girl gasping for air and needing to be rescued.

I get the mixed-up feelings, though, of being found out yet happy I can stop pretending. We are more alike than you know.

Because Two Are Better Than One

The girl who lives in my Google Maps app is awesome. Although much of the time she pronounces the names of streets I know like the back of my hand dreadfully wrong, she gets pretty much everything else right.

The other day I needed to get to a restaurant I had never been to before. It was across town, and of course it was rush hour and raining. Google Maps Girl was not at all stressed by these inconveniences. She told me there were several options I could take to get to my destination. One route, however, would be a bit faster because of traffic. I took her advice. During the drive, she told me in advance where to turn and which lane to get into when I turned onto a four-lane road. If that weren't enough to make me sing her praises, she let me know I was going to arrive at my destination early in spite of the traffic and the rain. I'm a girl who rarely arrives on time, so my early arrival was cause for a small dance party in my van as I pulled into the restaurant parking lot. (If only Google Maps Girl could find a way to get me caught up on my dishes. That would be even more awesome.)

Now, I know something about you simply because you picked up this book and started reading. I know you are a woman who feels fresh out of amazing. I know you are looking for answers. I know you are grateful that somebody else has said it aloud and you can raise your hand and say, "Me too."

But here is what I don't know: Which route did you take to get here? We don't all become fresh out of amazing the same way. Just like the Google Maps Girl tells me there are many ways to get to my destination, there are just as many ways to arrive at a place in your life where you feel you need to be amazing, but you are, frankly, fresh out.

What you will find in Part 1 are five different types of fresh-out-of-amazing girls. Each girl has taken a different route to get to that point, but the results are the same. Here is a quick glimpse of each one:

- **Burdened and Busy:** This fresh-out-of-amazing girl tries to be lots of people all at once, and she's not feeling particularly good about how she's doing any of them. She is trying hard to balance life as all these people. In the process, her life has fallen into much busyness, and she is not in sync or communion with God. This girl is overwhelmed and frazzled even though she may be doing everything right.

- **She's Amazing and I'm Not:** This girl has always felt fresh out of amazing. To make matters worse, everyone else is doing amazing things, and she is not. When will it be her turn to be amazing?

- **I Feel Like My Dreams Have Died:** This girl has a dream in her heart, but no matter what she does, she keeps coming up short. For reasons she can't explain, it seems like the answer is always no. This pattern can send a girl into a tailspin of "Why me?" because dreams that slip away hurt like crazy.

- **Liar, Liar, Pants on Fire:** This fresh-out-of-amazing girl has started believing the lies of the enemy. She has made fear her friend, and she is convinced the trial she's facing is going to defeat her.

- **When You've Lost Your Song in the Valley of Bitterness:** C.S. Lewis called pain a megaphone used by God to get our attention. After I turned in the manuscript for my first book, *Hope for the Weary Mom,* and completed a busy season of ministry, my dad died suddenly after a long battle with cancer. In the days and weeks that followed his death, "fresh out of amazing" took on new meaning for me. God had my attention and began to speak a new word of truth over my heart.

I have struggled in each of these areas because I am a bit of an overachiever. Maybe you will find glimpses of yourself in one particular chapter. I'm guessing you might really grab onto one chapter and say, "Hey, that's me!" But don't skip over the others. There are truths on every page for you and maybe for your best friend. So read it with her in mind too.

In this first section of the book, you will identify your core issues and take the beginning steps toward wholeness. Think of me as your very own Google Maps Girl. I will be there with you every step of the way. When we get to our destination, we will be ready for a deeper conversation because we have bonded. I just love that about road trips. Don't you? I don't even mind if you put your feet on the dashboard.

Part 2 is your invitation to move from being fresh out of amazing to gazing into the heart of Jesus. I will take you through a step-by-step process I believe will help you see that where you stand now is an opportunity and not the end of the world.

But we'll talk more about that later. For now, let's begin.

Chapter 1

Can This Fresh-Out-of-Amazing Girl Live?

Hurricane.

You have got to be kidding me, I thought.

I slid onto the floor next to a pile of three-day-old clean laundry. The television was muted with an afternoon talk show, and I was buried in every way. How was I going to manage surviving a literal storm when there was already one brewing inside me? I watched the public service announcement scroll across the screen. I was not amused.

I had been pushed to the brink the entire week. My husband had been out of the country on business for about two weeks, and—I have to be honest—I was not doing well. My youngest was almost two years old at the time, and her sleeping was not consistent. I was two years tired.

My oldest girls were excited because they had a special school event scheduled for the weekend. I was trying my best to share in their chatty exuberance, but I could not get on board. You see, they needed help with their book reports and their costumes for the schoolwide book ball. How could I not be proud of my girls who had worked hard all summer reading their favorite books? They were each planning lavish outfits so they would match a beloved character. In addition, their book reports needed to be edible. Cute, right?

Now, there are two things you need to know about me: I don't sew, and creative cooking is completely lost on me. I am lucky to get a meal on the table with at least two food groups each evening. So creating and executing a book report that people might want to eat was causing me to stress a bit.

I'll admit it: I was in my room, hiding from my responsibility and the girls' expectations when the television announced the impending storm. I had been through hurricanes before, but never when I was alone with my children. I think I started laughing nervously—and then the tears followed.

In that moment of desperation, I poured out my heart to Jesus. It felt like the storm inside me was pouring out. He met me in every way there on the floor and breathed hope over my weary soul. In the next few minutes I can't explain exactly what happened, but when I got up I felt better. I also knew without a shadow of doubt that he wanted me to write about what I was feeling. So I put this on my blog:

> I've pretty much fallen short in every category. I am tired
> and not really good for much right now. The trouble
> is, Lord, that I need to be amazing and I'm fresh out of
> amazing. At least it sure feels that way.[1]

For the first time in my life I put the words on a page and spoke them out loud: *I'm fresh out of amazing.*

I think somewhere deep inside I wished that hurricane would go ahead and blow right through and take me with it. At that point it wouldn't have taken much more than a gentle breeze to knock me over. I felt like a pile of dry, brittle bones that could easily be blown in every direction. I think the question swirling around my heart as the wind whipped up a mess outside sounded a lot like this: *Can a fresh-out-of-amazing girl live through this?*

In the days that followed, God literally and figuratively calmed the storm. The hurricane was downgraded, my girls' school event was canceled, and my husband returned home. Over the next three years God did an extraordinary hope-filled work in my life. But it was only the beginning.

Have you ever noticed how questions tend to boomerang back into our lives if we don't answer them soul-deep the first time? Recently, this nagging question—*Can a fresh-out-of-amazing girl live through this?*—came back around. God knows just the right time to have us revisit a lesson we need to learn in the worst way.

I think questions like this cry out for a lively discussion with a good friend, preferably over coffee and Panera Cinnamon Crunch bagels. So if we were sitting together today in my kitchen, I would start a pot of coffee and tell my kids to walk the dog to give us a few quiet moments. I am desperate to know what you think about this question. Once the coffee finished brewing and the kids were on their way, I would pour you a cup. Of course I would pour a cup for me as well, look you in the eye, and say, "Can this fresh-out-of-amazing girl live?"

I'm guessing you might look at me kind of funny and say, "Where did that question come from?" I would smile, take a sip of my over-creamed coffee, and say, "I'm so glad you asked. Let's talk about some dry bones, shall we?"

Dry Bones, the Bible, and What Happens When God Asks the Question

One reason I love the Bible is it answers the most critical questions we need to consider. It is also gloriously filled with everyday people like you and me who ask the same questions we do. Mothers, fathers, writers, farmers, Pharisees, sisters, fishermen, foreigners, and sinners grace the pages. You don't have to wade very far in to find someone who looks and thinks like you do.

Last week I found a reflection of my fresh-out-of-amazing self in a story about the prophet Ezekiel. Now he didn't use my language, but I think he might have appreciated it. He was in a pretty unique situation, and God showed up with a pep talk we can all benefit from. If you aren't familiar with Ezekiel, let me tell you what his Facebook profile might have read if he were alive today instead of 570 BC:

> Ezekiel: Pastor and prophet to exiled nation of Israel. I prefer to be a messenger of hope and comfort, but sometimes I have to tell it like it is. I see things like dry bones, and God talks to me. I love words, and I have been known to eat them.

But if Ezekiel had a Facebook profile, he wouldn't have many friends or likes on his status updates. Prophets were not always popular, as you can imagine. In Ezekiel 37 we get a glimpse of his life:

> The hand of the LORD was upon me, and he brought me out in the Spirit of the LORD and set me down in the middle of the valley; it was full of bones. And he led me around among them, and behold, there were very many on the surface of the valley, and behold, they were very dry (verses 1-2).

Although this type of thing probably didn't happen every day in his life, Ezekiel was accustomed to having visions and hearing God speak. So this journey to a field of dry bones probably didn't set him into panic mode as it might have done for me. If you suddenly find yourself in a valley filled with dry bones, I am not the person to call for help. Just ask my husband about the last time he took me to see a mildly scary movie. Nope, I don't do dry bones or seeing dead people of any kind. But Ezekiel did just fine with those bones.

The language in this scene is highly symbolic and richly layered with truth. God was literally grabbing hold of Ezekiel and inviting him to see something amazing. It was a God-directed work, something that only he could orchestrate. And at the very beginning God posed a question to Ezekiel to see if he knew the answer: "Son of man, can these bones live?" (verse 3). The question itself was rhetorical. God wasn't looking for the answer; he knew the answer. God wanted Ezekiel to declare with his own God-made mouth the truth he himself desperately needed to hear: "O Lord GOD, you know" (verse 3). Good answer, Ezekiel. Good answer. The truth is always, "O Lord GOD, you know," because he *does* know.

Next, God gave Ezekiel a short to-do list. The first item on the list was to prophesy over the bones, and the second was to prophesy to the breath. *To prophesy* here means "to pour forth words as with great emotion."[2] God didn't want Ezekiel to pour out any old words. He wanted Ezekiel to say this:

> O dry bones, hear the word of the LORD. Thus says the Lord GOD to these bones: Behold, I will cause breath to enter you, and you shall live (verses 4-5).

When Ezekiel obeyed, he saw God's living and active word take a pile of dry bones and resurrect an entire army. He witnessed the Spirit breathing life into those brittle bones. What was dead became alive because of the power of God.

Does that image give you chills too? Bones on the ground became an army ready for war! What can God *not* do?

<hr>

The truth is always, "O Lord,
GOD, you know," because he *does* know.

<hr>

I love what happened next: God explained the vision. How many times have you scratched your head and asked God, "What are you doing? Why do you want me to do this?" Ezekiel didn't have to wonder because God told him in great detail what the vision meant.

You see, God wasn't really concerned about a bunch of dry bones. Those bones represented the whole house of Israel, and God's heart was entirely focused on them, his people. They were captives broken by a brutal ruler who had destroyed their home in Jerusalem and left it in ruins. So God was moving toward his people in their agony. Israel said: "Our bones are dried up, our hope is gone, there's nothing left of us" (Ezekiel 37:11 MSG).

Dried up.

Hope is gone.

Nothing left of us.

Sounds like agony to me.

Don't you hate it when someone is telling you a story and, in the middle of it, starts telling you another story? They go off on a tangent, following a crazy rabbit trail, and you have no idea where they're headed. That can be frustrating. I promise you, though, you will not be frustrated with what I'm about to tell you. So let me push the "pause" button for a brief moment in this gripping dry bones story because of the four-letter word in this passage: hope.

I have made a habit of studying this word when I find it in Scripture. The definition of *tiqvah*, the Hebrew word for hope, is "cord, hope, expectation, things hoped for."[3] That the word is defined as "cord" puzzled me, so I did some research and found another place *tiqvah* appears in Scripture:

> Behold, when we come into the land, you shall tie this scarlet *cord* in the window through which you let us down, and you shall gather into your house your father and mother, your brothers, and all your father's household (Joshua 2:18).

This verse is from the account of a prostitute named Rahab who lived inside the wall of the city of Jericho. She hid the Israelite spies whom Joshua had sent to scout out the city. Her entire family was saved from utter destruction because of her kindness and courage.

During the siege upon the city, she was told to hang a cord—a *tiqvah* of scarlet—out her window. Anyone in her home at the time would be saved. She was to hang "hope" out her window and it would secure her salvation that day. Not only was her family saved, but they were grafted into the nation of Israel. Check the genealogy of Christ in Matthew and guess whose name you'll find. That's right—Rahab, the Canaanite prostitute who was saved when she hung up a scarlet cord called hope, is a relative of Jesus.

God's Word has the power to
resurrect and revive our lifeless hearts.

Now, back to our dry bones. The nation of Israel knew about Rahab and the scarlet cord called hope, but they had no such cord of hope to hold onto. Or did they? God's people felt cut off from him, but they weren't. God saw them, faint and discouraged, and he was going to restore them. They had not lost their cord of hope. They just couldn't see it.

Depleted and desperate, the people of Israel were now in a position to listen to God. Knowing that, God told Ezekiel he was going to do these things for Israel:

Resurrect: In Ezekiel 37:12, God said he was going to open the graves (of his people's hearts) and bring them back to life. How was God going to do this? By the power of his Word. God's Word has the power to resurrect and revive our lifeless hearts. I wonder if we truly understand the power God's Word has. Jesus affirmed this power when he said, "The Father can give life to those who are dead;

in the same way, the Son can give the gift of life to those He chooses" (John 5:21 THE VOICE). God was choosing to give the gift of life to Israel just when they needed it most.

Restore: Israel's restoration was inherently tied to the land God had promised them in his covenant with their forefather Abraham. Sitting in captivity in a foreign land, however, was utter defeat for them. God not only told Ezekiel that Israel would return to the land of his promise, but he also said, "I will carry you *straight* back to the land of Israel. Then you will know that I am the Eternal One" (Ezekiel 37:12 THE VOICE). God told the truth and proclaimed a promise he himself would bear the burden of fulfilling. Like a shepherd carrying a wandering lamb, God promised to carry his people in his arms to demonstrate to them he is Lord.

Renew: God was not yet finished with his hope-filled prophecy. He then promised to put his Spirit within his people and give them life. Offering this work of complete healing, God called them out of the graves with the power of his Word, he restored them to the Promised Land, and he breathed the breath of life into them. They could not breathe life into themselves. God would do this. This was a prophecy of great hope for a people who needed it as they sat captive in a foreign land. Through it God demonstrated he had not forgotten Israel, his covenant promise of being their God, or his loving-kindness to them. Their cord of hope—God Almighty—was not gone. He was holding onto them the whole time. He had spoken of his faithfulness, and he would be true to his Word.

God told the truth and proclaimed a promise he himself would bear the burden of fulfilling.

Back to My Kitchen Table

So, after telling you about dry bones and the bonus tangent story of Rahab and the cord of hope, I would refill your cup of coffee and say again, "Can this fresh-out-of-amazing girl live?" We would probably look at each other and then look down at our coffee and pray the kids would burst in and save us from having to answer. Fresh out of amazing feels heavy. And it can be hard to talk about. We might imagine right there at my table the dry bones covering us six feet deep. Still, both of us would have a choice to make. Regardless of our choice, the truth would still be, "Only God knows."

God knows what we need when our own bones are dry and our hope seems lost. We need to hear from him, do what he says, and then watch his restorative work in our lives. We need to trust his Spirit to revive us. Friends, fresh-out-of-amazing girls are objects of God's grace too. He wants to move in our lives in ways we can't imagine. And we will not be able to point to crafty words, winning strategies, or brilliant performances when he is finished. We will point to him.

Can this fresh-out-of-amazing girl live? Only God knows. This is what he does.

How God Renovates Our Hearts

I've never remodeled an old house, but I love to watch those fixer-upper programs on television. First, the host shows the prospective buyers a home that is in a pretty horrible state. He tells them to look beyond the ugly because it has stunning potential.

The buyers can see some obvious problems. They know going into the deal that the house needs to be repainted and refloored—and for goodness' sake! The 1970s called and wants its avocado-green kitchen back. The couple takes the risk and makes the purchase for pennies on the dollar.

Inevitably, after the renovations are underway, they find major structural issues that need to be addressed. The homeowners seem shocked that their fixer-upper truly needed more than cosmetic changes. Suddenly their investment looks more like a money pit. About midpoint during the show, they despair...only to cry tears of joy later when they see their home reborn. As it turns out, they were in the great hands of their master builder, and now they have the home they always dreamed of.

Hearts are like homes. Our hearts have doors and walls and rooms filled with every aspect of life. If you looked at mine in the past few years you would see the façade of one weary and worn woman doing her best to choose hope every day. As I began to write about hope and live out the truths God was teaching me, I saw real change in myself. Others did too. But, with every truth I applied, God revealed more work I needed to complete at a deeper heart level.

Fresh-out-of-amazing girls are
objects of God's grace too.

God has indeed met me in my mess, but my fixer-upper heart needed a complete remodel. My foundation had cracked under the weight of other people's expectations, my walls were covered with to-do lists, and my wiring was outdated by the idea that I was responsible for everything. God was whispering to me. Really, it was more like a calling I could hear in the distance. It echoed louder as the days passed, but I had no clue where to begin the demolition process. I just knew the project was about to get messier.

Years ago I thought that once we passed through a trial or a test we moved on to the next thing. But lately I've begun to realize you don't move on; you move inward. God just keeps putting his finger on an issue that needs deeper work because he cares that deeply. He has the good intention to not just do a temporary cosmetic fix. God wants a heart-level overhaul. He desires our maturity more than just our maintenance.

Maybe you can relate to the mess I'm talking about. You think you are doing pretty well because God has been doing business in one key area of your life. You honestly believe you are about to have a breakthrough when suddenly it feels more like a breakdown. I have found that the Master Builder of our lives is ever patient and thorough. We can find great confidence in this truth: "He who began a good work in you will bring it to completion at the day of Jesus Christ" (Philippians 1:6).

1. He begins the work. We can't possibly begin the work ourselves. So, in his great wisdom, God starts the process. Left to my own accord, I would rather sit and drink my coffee every morning and read a fashion magazine instead of reading his Word, praying, and inviting him to move in my life. I know the work God wants to do in me is not going to be comfortable. Works of his grace rarely are—and that work gets messier before it gets better. Songwriter and worship leader Kristene DiMarco says, "Anything inspired by the Holy Spirit will always be dripping with hope."[4] Girls, no matter how messy it gets, the outcome is worth the mess—and there is always hope.

God wants a heart-level overhaul. He desires our maturity more than just our maintenance.

2. He completes the work. Is it any wonder God is committed to the work he begins? He does not abandon us once the walls begin to come down. He will not leave us demolished and hopeless.

Matthew Henry said, "We may be confident, or well persuaded, that God not only will not forsake, but that he will finish and crown the work of his own hands. For, as for God, his work is perfect."[5]

I don't really think we want him to do a half-baked job. We want to be perfected but we want it on our terms. We know what we want but we don't quite know how to get there. But God does. He has the vision and we simply need to lean into that work. It is always in our best interest to let God work in us until he is finished.

3. He has a goal with eternity in mind. A promise has a powerful pull, and this verse includes the promise of completion on the day when Jesus comes to set all things in this upside-down world right. That day is yet to be. So it would seem to follow that the work God has begun in our lives may take more time than we would like to give it. But a promise is a promise. We can be sure that a slow-to-be-fulfilled (from our perspective) promise is still a promise.

God is willing to pour all that he is into our lives because on the day when Jesus comes back to claim us, we will be ready. Tears of joy may break forth when we see what God was building in us all along. We will be the dream he knew we could be. He will have labored over every nook and cranny, and then his work will be complete.

Doesn't this New Testament promise remind you of what God said to Ezekiel? "I will cause breath to enter you, and you shall live" (Ezekiel 37:5). Scripture always supports Scripture and this truth is confirmed here. We will know that our resurrection, restoration, and renewal are his work, and we will know by his work that he is the Lord.

What If I'm Not Fresh Out of Amazing Yet?

When I first started writing *Hope for the Weary Mom* with my friend Brooke, someone asked us if we minded being known as "those weary moms." I realized in that moment that not every mom would call herself weary. Oh, maybe she finds herself having weary moments, but she would not define herself as a mom who tends to be overwhelmed by life and the ordinary days that mothering often strings together.

Many moms live just slightly above the place I would call weary. God makes each of us unique, and he works in our lives in a thousand different ways. My weary-mom world may not resonate with every mom, and I'm okay with that.

The same can be said about being fresh out of amazing. Maybe you picked up this book because you liked the cover or your best friend told you to read it. (Bless her if she did.) Perhaps, though, at this point of chapter 1, you are wondering if this message is for you. Quite frankly, you are not in a fresh-out-of-amazing place. You are actually doing pretty well. Your hope is firmly in place. You are chasing your dreams and have all the faith you think you need for the days ahead. You may actually feel amazing today.

Goodness, that makes me so happy for you, and I truly do wish you were sitting in my kitchen with me. I need people like you in my life more than you know. This past year I prayed that God would send me just those types of friends to encourage my heart. He was so faithful to do that. These girls invited me to lunch, bought me coffee, and showed up to cheer me on. God sent real live friends into my life to encourage me. Has he done that for you too?

But here is something you might consider before you put this book back on the shelf or tell your best friend *thanks but no thanks*. Maybe you aren't reading for yourself today. Could it be that God wants to give you words for a sister-friend who needs you to speak truth to her? Is it your turn to show up with coffee for a fresh-out-of-amazing sister who simply needs a hug and a good word?

I like to think there is something for every girl in this book. I have done my best to walk through the pages of God's Word and tell stories that I think will encourage you no matter where you are today. You don't have to be in the depths of despair to read this book or like it. You might find you have only moments here and there when you feel fresh out of amazing. I believe God wants to enter those moments—and he can do more than you can imagine with a moment we surrender to him.

You might also want to keep this idea in mind as you continue to read: Fresh out of amazing can sneak up on you and plant itself squarely in your life without any warning signs. Perhaps there is a bit of that just around the bend of the road waiting for you that you simply can't see. This book might be one way God is preparing your heart for that season. If that is the case, do me a favor. Don't resist this part of the journey. Heart preparation is always beneficial and worth our time. I like what Dr. Billy Graham said: "Mountaintops are for views and inspiration, but fruit grows in the valley."[6] If this is your time on the mountaintop, I pray you will be inspired. But if it is time for growing fruit in the valley, let's get on with it and see what God has in store for us.

I'm Ready. Are You?

Writer and speaker Lysa TerKeurst said, "I started this message with the need to live this message." My friend, this is where I am today. I'm willing to work my way through this message and see where God leads. Such God-initiated, God-completed work in my heart is necessary. I don't know about you, but I'm ready. The Lord has been dropping all kinds of hints that it is time to find a once-and-for-all solution for this familiar place. That solution will begin and end with him.

I'd love to have the honor of walking with you as well. I find the best place to start any new journey is with a word of prayer. I'll share mine with you, or you can pen your own. Either way, it is time for dry bones to live. Jesus won't leave us. We have the promise he will carry us home. Complete.

Lord,

When I'm fresh out of amazing, I feel as though I am just like a pile of dry and brittle bones. Lifeless. Desperate.

And you ask, "Can this fresh-out-of-amazing girl live?" I look at you and say, "Only you know, Lord. Only you know." Because there is nothing left in me, it has to be you.

Jesus, you said, "The words that I have spoken to you are spirit and life." Lord, send your life-giving Word. Where I see hopelessness, show me possibility. When I feel cut off, draw near. You open the grave of my heart, and you revive me. You restore. I am blessed by your grace.

Let my life be a testimony so that others see and know you are God.

Amen

Chapter 2

Burdened and Busy

I've been trying to find the time to sit down and write this chapter, but I've been too busy. And it's the kind of busy I can't quit either. Most of it has involved driving. I needed to drive my oldest daughter to several drama rehearsals. Another one of my girls had to go to the doctor. All of them needed to be fed, of course, and that involved grocery shopping and cooking. You get the idea, right?

The irony is not lost on me: I'm too busy to write about being busy. Who says the Lord doesn't have a sense of humor? He does, and he often uses it to remind me that he has his eye on me all the time.

I am writing on this topic for a reason: I need it in the worst way—and I need it today. I am writing and learning right along with you. I'm not speaking to you as someone who has it all figured out or deserves a badge with "Expert" on it. No, I'm as nervous as you are as we get started. In fact, it feels like the first day of middle school all over again: *Am I wearing the right shirt? Does my lip gloss match? Should my jeans be cuffed and rolled or just loose on the outside of my tennis shoes?* Somebody please say, "Bless that girl" and let's get started before I chicken out altogether.

Busy and Responsible

When I was a little girl, I had a book called *The Ant and the Grass-hopper*. My version of this Aesop's Fable was published by Disney, and Jiminy Cricket played the grasshopper. (Maybe that's why to this day I don't know the difference between crickets and grasshoppers.) Do you know the story? The little ant is busy and responsible, constantly working and storing up food for winter. The grasshopper uses his time for sloth and leisure. He is the life of every picnic. The ant will have no part of it. As the weather turns colder, the grasshopper realizes his mistake. He is left out in the cold with nothing to eat. Lucky for him—at least in the Disney version—the ant invites him into his cozy home, and the grasshopper survives the winter.

I wore that book out with all my "Daddy, read it to me again" requests. I think my pleading probably wore him out too, but he always said yes. One night he added this extra moral to the story: "If you want to get something accomplished, ask a busy person and it will get done." I knew he was right. I grew up with determination to never be that lazy grasshopper Jiminy Cricket. I would work hard. I would be busy with being busy. I would be responsible like the ant, and I would try to treat lazy grasshoppers with kindness and grace. Growing up, others would describe me as *dependable, teacher's pet, obedient*, and *conscientious*. You might say I was a good girl. I certainly would.

Years later I took a test to discover my strengths. I discovered—not surprisingly—that responsibility is one of my top five strengths. This is how StrengthsFinder 2.0 put it: "Your responsibility theme forces you to take psychological ownership for anything you commit to, and whether large or small, you feel emotionally bound to follow it through to completion. Your good name depends on it."[1]

Yes, I can identify with that. Words like *ownership, emotionally bound*, and her *name depends on it* resonate deeply with me.

Do those words fit you as well? Maybe like me, you see our sense of responsibility as a good thing. People would say I'm dependable.

Others would say they like working with me. My husband knows that on most nights he can trust the house not to be a complete war zone and dinner to be on the table before 7:00 p.m. Now, sometimes dinner is frozen pizza or pancakes, but he knows some food will be there. My kids know that if I tell them I will pick them up from school, I will be there. I might not be early, but I will always come.

StrengthsFinder continues: "This conscientiousness, this near obsession for doing things right, and your impeccable ethics, combine to create your reputation: utterly dependable."[2] This serves us well for the most part. We like being utterly dependable because—let's face it—it is better than the alternative.

But what happens when our sense of responsibility gets out of control and takes over our lives? StrengthsFinder does say "near obsession," right? My sense of responsibility is a strength, but it has the potential of becoming a weakness of epic proportions. How does this happen? Well, for starters I start to feel responsible for all things. Not just the people and projects in my life. I begin to feel like I am responsible for how people—who aren't my people—act and feel. I have guilt over not saying yes to every invitation to serve. Do you know what I mean? Do you:

- Read Facebook and feel bad for all the bad in the world? Do you hurt over thinking you should be the one to fix it all?

- Lie awake at night worried and not sleeping?

- Fret over decisions you made that others might not understand?

- Feel paralyzed by the thought that you let someone down?

- Find yourself continually running around tending to all the things on your to-do list and having no time for soul rest?

- Battle the feeling of being constantly overwhelmed?
- Sit down? Ever?

My sense of responsibility leads me to care about people and situations, and most of the time that is a blessing. But caring should not always lead to doing. Read what Kevin DeYoung wrote about that fact:

> Care is not the same as do. At the Lausanne missions gathering in 2010, John Piper made the statement, "We should care about all the suffering, especially eternal suffering." He chose the word "care" quite carefully. He didn't want to say we should *do* something about all the suffering, because we can't do something about everything. But we can care.[3]

Our sense of responsibility can and should lead us to care. But doing is optional. Besides, we can only do so much.

Now, if you're like me, you might need to let this truth sit in your heart for a minute. You may be saying, "What? Doing is optional? And I can only do so much?" Friend, I know that as a responsible person you can do a lot. In fact, you can do more than most people. God made you this way, but he also set divine limitations on us. In his wisdom, God only gave us twenty-four hours each day, two hands, and one mouth. We can't be all things to all people. Even though we certainly have days when we believe we can. We both know that when our gift—our sense of responsibility—is out of control, we become busy, burdened, and fresh out of amazing. We might find ourselves steps away from throwing up our hands and quitting life altogether because quitting is so much better than failing. Trust me, friend. This message is for me too.

Sometimes, instead of making me want to quit, my sense of responsibility can make me downright bossy and annoyed with needy people who are less responsible than I am. Does that make you grimace a bit? That sentence was hard for me to write, but I'm being honest with you. A woman stretched thin has a temper to match. Responsibility can cause me to be overwhelmed to the point that I become pretty hard to live with. Ask my kids. Wait a minute! On second thought, don't ask my kids. Seriously, do you ever imagine that, on one of your worst days, a film crew is secretly recording your every moment? You know the moment I'm talking about. The moment you start to...uh...say things very loudly. You become the responsible yeller because if you speak loudly enough, everyone around you will see that you are the one doing all the work. *You* are making life happen. *You* are getting it done. Alone.

I remember hearing Oprah talk about some poor woman's "moment" on her talk show. She said, "Can you believe she said *that* to her kids?" The audience was horrified. They were shocked any human being could yell such a thing. Meanwhile, I was hugging my knees as I sat in my chair thinking, *Didn't I just say pretty much the same thing ten minutes ago?* Oh, friends, we've all been there. I'm thinking even Oprah herself has been, but I'm just speculating.

I know one woman who has definitely been there. This woman wasn't on Oprah's show. Instead, her moment was recorded in the Bible in black and white for all of us to witness and throw our stones at and be horrified by her behavior. But you know what? She is an awful lot like me.

Martha: Her Name Is Hanging in the Air

You knew we had to go there, didn't you? Her name is hanging in the air like excessive amounts of perfume in the cosmetic department at Macy's. Perfume is sweet in small amounts. Mix several together, and you get too much of a good thing.

Martha is the girl for the burdened and busy crowd. If we had a Christian magazine for the fresh-out-of-amazing woman, Martha would grace the cover more than the Kardashians do the cover of *People*. We would shake our heads at her and say under our breath,

"I'm not surprised" as we put our groceries on the conveyer and glance sideways at the cover so our kids don't see us. We expect Martha to behave that way. We love to hate her, but we are like her in so many ways. Martha is a mirror who reflects our image. We find ourselves bothered and drawn to her peculiar struggle. I think it is time we take a good long look in the mirror she offers us.

Luke 10:38-42 tells the story of Martha and her sister Mary. Many people like to call Martha the "don't" in the story and hold up Mary as a beautiful "do." But you and I get Martha in a way not everyone does. "She is our people," as my friend Brooke would say. Let's not abandon our dear sister in the kitchen from the beginning. I am grateful Martha is real, raw, and uncut from the pages of God's Word. I think it is powerful for us fresh-out-of-amazing girls to take an honest look at what Martha did, what she said, and how Jesus responded to her. I think in the process we might hear Jesus calling our names as well.

What Fresh-Out-of-Amazing Martha Did

Martha welcomed Jesus. Friends, this is no small thing. Jesus came to her house as a demonstration (most likely) of his teaching earlier in the chapter on how the disciples were to go about preaching the gospel.

> When you enter a house seeking lodging, say, "Peace on this house!" If a child of peace—one who welcomes God's message of peace—is there, your peace will rest on him. If not, don't worry; nothing is wasted. Stay where you're welcomed. *Become part of the family,* eating and drinking whatever they give you (Luke 10:5-7 The Voice).

A few paragraphs later in the text, Jesus entered Martha's home and "a woman named Martha welcomed him into her house" (Luke 10:38). The passage doesn't say that Martha's sister Mary welcomed

Jesus or that their brother Lazarus welcomed Jesus. The house may have belonged to Martha. If that's the case, it makes sense that, when Jesus entered her home, she welcomed him. He became part of her family when he entered. This meant Jesus, along with his friends who were with him, entered Martha's home, and she was to perform the hospitable duties of the day. She fed them and made them feel like family.

And Martha's hospitality was no small gesture. Consider the cost of welcoming Jesus into her home, the first and most obvious being financial. I know how much my four girls and my husband eat during a usual meal. Can you imagine feeding thirteen hungry preacher men? But without hesitation, Martha welcomed them into her home. Their visit also cost Martha her reputation with the local religious leaders as well as her neighbors. Jesus and his followers were growing more and more unpopular. It was becoming risky for locals to be seen with them, let alone feed them and treat them like family. Still, Martha welcomed them all into her home.

So, before we pick apart Martha's actions, let's consider she did a whole lot right too. I think that's because Martha not only had the gift of hospitality, but a strong sense of responsibility as well. She welcomed these men of God because welcoming people was what she always did. Feeling it was her role and (we can relate) her responsibility, she took care of people. I think Martha cared deeply about her friend Jesus, and she demonstrated that by opening her home and heart to him and his followers. I believe she loved loving people this way. She was, by nature, a servant serving.

But. Martha's story has a *but.* Every story has one. For example, I am passionate about walking with God and doing what his Word says, but many times I don't do those things. Daily I find myself in messes of my own making. Praise the Lord that something is working in my favor, and that something is the grace of God. We are about to see that same grace at work in Martha's story.

I really wish we could push the "pause" button, step into the story, put an arm around Martha, and say, "Girl, I understand, but let's not be here in the kitchen like this. Let's not have a *but* interrupting your beautiful welcome of Jesus." Yet here it is: "But Martha was distracted with much serving" (Luke 10:40).

The Message translation says, "But Martha was pulled away [from Jesus] by all she had to do in the kitchen." And her busyness gave rise to anxiety. Right there in her kitchen, with Jesus sitting a few feet away, busyness was beating Martha up one side and down another. Consumed by all she had to do, Martha was about to have a moment. She was probably in the kitchen stirring a pot of something wonderful, and she was getting herself all stirred up too. Martha was about to blow a fuse, and she was going to tell one person in particular all about it.

What Fresh-Out-of-Amazing Martha Said

> She went up to [Jesus] and said, "Lord, do you not care that my sister has left me to serve alone? Tell her then to help me" (Luke 10:40).

Martha not only interrupted Jesus as he taught, but she asked him flat out if he cared about her: *Don't you care, Jesus? Don't you care?* Then she told Jesus what to do. Yes, she did. Have mercy! *Fresh-out-of-amazing girl done told Jesus to tell Mary to help her.* I die a little at this point. Do you know why? Because I sound like her just about every other day around 5:00 p.m. when my kids are hungry, impatient, and ready for dinner. I slam all the doors, I crash all the pots, and I blow my fuse too. I tell everyone within a room or two of my voice all the things I'm doing all by myself. I tell them I have had it. I mean *had it.*

What I really want my girls to say as they jump up to help me is, "Oh, Mom, you are so awesome! Look at how much you are doing for us because you love us. Let us help you and make your life easier." But most of the time, they stare at me blankly and continue with their lives, pretending that my tantrum never happened. In their defense, if they did offer to help, I would probably refuse. Only one Person can help me when I am at my breaking point, and that Person is exactly who Martha went to with her problem: Martha told Jesus. (At least she has that going for her!)

I think Martha really wanted Jesus to swing into action on her behalf and solve her immediate problem. Jesus had a greater good to do for her, though. He was looking right at her heart, and he knew there was a more important issue at hand.

Martha's fresh-out-of-amazing moment took her to the feet of Jesus, but instead of savoring his presence, she pouted. Martha was busy, but she didn't have to be burdened.

Jesus's Response to Fresh-Out-of-Amazing Martha

I love that fresh-out-of-amazing girls like us have a chance to witness how Jesus responded to Martha. I think we can learn a lot by looking at what Jesus said to her:

> Martha, Martha, you are anxious and troubled about many things, but one thing is necessary. Mary has chosen the good portion, which will not be taken away from her (Luke 10:41-42).

Let's break down what Jesus said:

- "Martha, Martha." Jesus repeated himself to get her attention. He spoke earnestly to her. He was not speaking to Mary, Peter, or John. He was speaking to Martha.

- "You are anxious and troubled about many things." Jesus realized Martha was distracted and disquieted by not one thing but by many. Yet the core issue was not that she had many things to do, but that she was letting those things pull her away from what was important.

- "Mary has chosen the good portion." Mary faced the same choice Martha did, and she chose to sit with Jesus and let him serve her his Word. His truth would not be taken from her in this moment or ever.

I think when Jesus spoke these words to Martha, he absolutely spoke them with love. Matthew Henry remarked, "There were some who were Christ's particular friends, whom he loved more than his other friends, and them he visited most frequently. He *loved* this family and often invited himself to them. Christ's visits are the tokens of his love."[4] Jesus showed that he cared for Martha by drawing out the real reason for her anxiety.

I think Jesus saw that Martha's heart was to serve and love those in her home. The problem arose when that became her primary focus instead of connecting with Jesus in the moment. Martha could have been in the kitchen blessing God for giving her the chance to cook for his Son. Instead of grumbling, she could have chosen to listen to what was being shared around the table as Jesus taught. She might have served out of an overflow of the love she had for Jesus. Martha's fresh-out-of-amazing moment took her to the feet of Jesus, but instead of savoring his presence, she pouted. Martha was busy, but she didn't have to be burdened. After all, this same Jesus who sat a few feet away from her while she boiled over with frustration also said this:

Are you tired? Worn out? Burned out on religion? Come
to me. Get away with me and you'll recover your life.
I'll show you how to take a real rest. Walk with me and
work with me—watch how I do it. Learn the unforced
rhythms of grace. I won't lay anything heavy or ill-fitting
on you. Keep company with me and you'll learn to live
freely and lightly (Matthew 11:28-30 msg).

What Martha needed—goodness! I need it every single day—
was to learn the Lord's unforced rhythms of grace. Martha could
have lived free instead of fresh out of amazing. This was Jesus's invitation to her.

We don't get to see what happened next, and that drives me a bit
crazy. I want to know…Did she cry? Did Jesus hug her? Did he walk
into the kitchen with her, tie a towel around his waist, and help her
serve like he did at the Last Supper? He might have done that here
too. We don't know.

A heart full of duty is no comparison
to a heart full of devotion.

Sometime later we catch another glimpse of Martha, this time
in a much different setting. Her beloved brother had died, and after
she had waited for Jesus for a few days, he came. Scripture tells us
that "when Martha heard that Jesus was coming, she went and met
him, but Mary remained seated in the house" (John 11:20). In the
aftermath of Lazarus's death, Martha went to Jesus first, before Mary
even stirred from her seat. Martha must have learned something
during Jesus's earlier visit. She didn't pull inward and let bitterness

get the best of her busy and burdened heart. I think she learned that keeping company with Jesus brings light and life to any and every situation. In fact, I think running to meet Jesus that day, she was counting on it.

Lainie's Story

My friend Angie moved here from Texas a few years ago. She has a best friend named Lainie whom she left behind in the Lone Star State. I have only met Lainie in real life once, but we are now friends too. She is the type of girl who says, "If you are Angie's friend, then you are mine." Lately, I've been talking to her about being fresh out of amazing, and she shared something with me that I think is so true of all us burdened and busy girls.

Lainie learned to "Martha" at a young age. She had the gift of service, and this was especially clear to her dad. She was a lot like him. When Lainie's mother became quite ill, her dad depended heavily on Lainie to help make life around the house run smoothly. By the age of thirteen, she was cooking dinner and taking care of everyone in the house—and she was pretty good at it. It didn't matter that she was only in seventh grade and had math homework to complete. Like Martha, Lainie was a servant serving, and doing so brought her joy.

Fast forward a few years, and Lainie was sitting in church, about to hear her first sermon on Martha. She was a bit excited because she knew for sure she could relate to being busy in the kitchen and taking care of people. But as the message unfolded, Lainie began to feel like her acts of service and busyness made her a failure. She began to wonder if maybe because she was not like Mary, she didn't really love Jesus enough. Whether the message was delivered with this intention or not, Lainie could not say. Clearly, she heard that she needed to leave behind her Martha ways and just be more like Mary.

This conclusion troubled her for years, and Lainie found herself fresh out of amazing under the burden of legalism and a whole lot of "should" talk: *You should be more spiritual. You should act a certain way. You should be more like Mary.* All that "should" talk can be exhausting, but God was faithfully in pursuit of Lainie's heart. She began to slowly understand this truth from Romans 8:1-2: "There is therefore now no condemnation for those who are in Christ Jesus. For the law of the Spirit of life has set you free in Christ Jesus from the law of sin and death."

Lainie realized she was not under condemnation from the Lord, and she was set free to be who God made her to be. She could still be a servant like Martha, but she could first be filled up like Mary. While she was working, she could find ways to be connected to Jesus and never have to be empty. Receiving his grace moment by moment made a huge difference. It even brought the joy back to her service. She learned that a heart full of duty is no comparison to a heart full of devotion.

One way Lainie fills up her heart while she is serving is by worshipping the Lord throughout the day. Lainie loves to sing, and her favorite hymn is called "I Must Tell Jesus." She could not have picked a better song to be her Martha anthem. It was written by a pastor named Elisha Hoffman in 1893 after he visited a weary mom who had experienced deep sorrow and suffering. Try as he might, no Scriptures Pastor Hoffman shared with her made a difference. In a moment of desperation, he said the best thing she could do would be to tell the Lord all of her sorrows. "You must tell Jesus," he told her.

While she was meditating on these words, a light broke across her face, and she cried, "Yes, I must tell Jesus."[5] Hoffman went home and wrote:

> I must tell Jesus all of my trials,
> I cannot bear these burdens alone;
> In my distress He kindly will help me,
> He ever loves and cares for His own.[6]

This song echoes the truth from 1 Peter 5:7: "[Cast] all your anxieties on him, because he cares for you." Friends, when we are fresh out of amazing, Jesus cares. He does not want us disquieted. His heart for us is tender. He speaks our names once, twice, or more in order to reconnect our souls to his. Jesus will help us. Jesus alone.

Chapter 3

She's Amazing and I'm Not

When I first wrote the words *fresh out of amazing* on my blog a few years ago, I felt like I was the only one in the entire world who thought she needed to be amazing and was fresh out. I was further convinced when I googled the phrase, and my name and blog post came up as the number-one response. According to Google, I also held the number two, three, and four spots for *fresh out of amazing*. Yes. I am fresh out of amazing, and Google proves it.

It came as a complete shock that other women felt the same way I did because, based on my observations of the women all around me, they were actually doing pretty amazing things. They were feeding their kids homegrown organic vegetables—and the kids actually ate them. (Seriously. How do they do that?) Their homes looked like a staged *Better Homes and Garden* photo shoot all the time. (Mine has some good days, but mostly it looks like a Barbie bomb went off in a busy fast-food restaurant.) To top it all off, they were traveling all over the world doing very exciting things while my life was really just a mix of mundane trips to the grocery store and across town to church. Every status update and blog post I read from other people sure seemed to point to the truth I felt so deeply: she's amazing and I am not.

As it turned out, I was not the only one feeling this way, the only one living with the tension of needing to be amazing and feeling fresh out. I didn't see that my experience greatly resonated with other women as well. When I stepped out of my comfort zone and waved my white flag and said, "I am not amazing—and I don't feel amazing," a whole lot of other women waved their white flags too and said, "Amen." It wasn't just weary moms either. Women of all sorts said they could identify with my words. I was in good company, and I'd had no idea.

Isn't that just like the enemy of our souls to convince us of such things? The same one who first said to Eve, "Did God really say not to eat from that tree?" also makes a habit of whispering in our ears, "You are the only one who feels this way. You'd better hide it for the rest of your life because if you tell others, they will think you are crazy." His lies fuel our fears. But the truth is, speaking such feelings out loud actually gives women permission to nod their heads in agreement and say, "Me too."

Feeling fresh out of amazing allowed the curse of comparison to move into my heart. I've learned that comparison runs deep in God's daughters. And it runs deep in my soul too. There are many days I wish I could speak a magic spell over my life and make myself the woman I've always wanted to be. This truth is beautifully illustrated in one of my favorite scenes in the film of *The Voyage of the Dawn Treader,* one of C.S. Lewis's Chronicles of Narnia. Lucy wanted to be beautiful like her older sister, Susan. She wanted it so badly that she almost wished her life away with fancy words—"An infallible spell that makes you she, the beauty you've always wanted to be."

Aslan, the wise hero of the story, tells her, "Your brothers and sisters wouldn't know Narnia without you, Lucy. You discovered it first, remember?" In wanting what her sister had, Lucy lost her childlike joy. She forgot who she was and entered an ugly place. She is drawn back by Aslan's words, "You doubt your value. Don't run from who you are."[1]

Fresh-out-of-amazing girls doubt their value too. They are experts at running from who they truly are and finding a million different ways they don't measure up to other women. I think we have a severe case of limited perspective. We also make the mistake of comparing our messy places to the cleaned-up versions of other people's messy places. Women have been doing this from the beginning of time.

A Tale of Two Sisters

I know a thing or two about sisters. Not that I have any myself, but I'm raising four girls and praying like crazy that God makes these sisters friends. Seldom does a day go by when one of them reminds me that some prayers are prayed again and again and again before we see evidence of God working.

As you can imagine, our lives are wordy and dramatic. More than once a day I hear the words "That isn't fair!" regarding some special treatment one sister thinks another has received. Still, I have no doubt God is working in the hidden places of their hearts. Relationships crafted over a lifetime of shared bathrooms, passing bread, and piling into the minivan for church sometimes take their toll. They aren't easy. But they are worth it.

One of the first relationships between women the Bible documents is that of Rachel and Leah, two sisters. You can find their story in Genesis 29 and 30 under the simple title "Jacob Marries Leah and Rachel." Notice anything potentially dramatic about this setup? If it doesn't cause you to wonder what in the world is going on, it certainly will by the time we are finished observing their lives. Maybe we can learn a thing or two from them because we are like them in so many ways.

> Laban had two daughters. The name of the older was Leah, and the name of the younger was Rachel. Leah's eyes were weak, but Rachel was beautiful in form and appearance (Genesis 29:16-17).

We learn quickly that Laban had two very different daughters. His oldest daughter was named Leah and her eyes were weak. It probably didn't matter how much she batted her eyelashes. Rachel, on the other hand, was gorgeous in every way. She was everything her sister was not. Can you imagine what kind of friction this might have caused between these two sisters? Understandably, Rachel was the one Jacob, the kinsman suitor, had eyes for. He was taken by her the first time he saw her.

After Jacob had been at Laban's for a month, he was asked, "What shall your wages be?" Jacob's response was "I will serve you seven years for your younger daughter Rachel" (Genesis 29:15,18). Jacob did exactly that, and those years "seemed to him but a few days because of the love he had for [Rachel]." Yep, this could have been the beginning of the perfect Hallmark movie. If only we could just omit the next few verses. But we can't.

> Laban gathered together all the people of the place and made a feast. But in the evening he took his daughter Leah and brought her to Jacob, and he went in to her (Genesis 29:22-23).

We should really pause for a second and let this scene sink deep down.

One sister thinks she is going to marry a man who was willing to work seven years for her hand. She must have been anticipating the wedding feast for years. Surely she had dreams and plans for how it would be magical in every way. Only she woke up and found out her fiancé had been duped into marrying her older sister.

And what of the older sister? Did she cry herself to sleep during those seven years, wondering when someone would come along and fall head over heels for her? Did she see her sister Rachel with Jacob and wonder, *When will it be my turn?* In a moment of deception she became part of a story we want to turn our heads away from and gasp, "No!" But Leah herself may have been deceived. Maybe her father told her what was going on, or maybe she believed for a moment or two it was really her turn to be favored for a change. She woke up in the morning still unlovely and unloved with one angry husband. Bless her. Don't you want to hug the hurt right out of her heart?

Their father Laban excused it all with a shrug of his shoulders and the statement that giving away the younger sister as a bride before the older is not done in his country. Then he offered to make a deal with Jacob:

> "Complete the [wedding] week of this one, and we will give you the other [sister] also in return for serving me another seven years." Jacob did so, and completed [Leah's] week. Then Laban gave him his daughter Rachel to be his wife (Genesis 29:27-28).

So here stands the family of Jacob: He now has two wives who are sisters sharing his tent, and he clearly loves one of them more than the other. (Seriously, can you believe this stuff is in the Bible?)

When our hearts are full of longing, we
fresh-out-of-amazing girls often can't see
blessings of others except as a cross to bear.
We feel pierced by their prize. We bleed and
we wonder why no one sees or cares.

Are you cheering for Team Leah or Team Rachel? Maybe at times you can empathize with both of them. My heart breaks for both of these women. I believe both Leah and Rachel are fresh out of amazing. They fall into the same trap of the curse of comparison, and, given free rein in their lives, it breeds sin. Of course there is more to the story. We really want to pull for one sister or another, but the best question to ask is, "Where is God in all of this mess?"

> When the LORD saw that Leah was hated, he opened her womb, but Rachel was barren. And Leah conceived and bore a son, and she called his name Reuben, for she said, "Because the LORD has looked upon my affliction; for now my husband will love me" (Genesis 29:31-32).

Leah was seen after all. God heard her certain weeping long into the night and gave her the gift of children. Not only did she have children, but she had sons. In fact, she had many sons. One of those sons, Judah, was in the lineage of Christ. God would work through Leah's broken and messy story of heartbreak to redeem the sins of the world. I love how *The Jesus Storybook Bible* paints this picture:

> When Leah knew that God loved her, in her heart it didn't matter anymore whether her husband loved her best, or if she was the prettiest. Someone had chosen her, someone did love her—with a Never Stopping, Never Giving Up, Unbreaking, Always and Forever Love.[2]

When we are fresh out of amazing, God does not look at us and say, "Wow, I have nothing to work with here." Instead, he bends down, he listens to our hearts, and he shows himself faithful.

But what about Rachel? Sure, she was loved by Jacob, but she was barren. Her wound may have been deeper than Leah's. My friend Sara knows the depth of an empty womb and says this: "Barrenness is about what you don't have so it's often undetected. I was sick— my body wasn't working—but I didn't have crutches or a sling. I just had my waistline, unmoving.[3]

Rachel sat with her waistline unmoving and watched as Leah birthed new life again and again. In Rachel's mind, the love Jacob had for her was small and insignificant by comparison to Leah's

She's Amazing and I'm Not   57

situation. So Rachel grew angry and demanded Jacob give her children. When he rightly pointed out that he was not God and had no control over such things, Rachel herself played god. She handed her husband a replacement and took the fruit of their union as her own.

Such taking matters into our own hands does not satisfy the longing in our hearts. Matthew Henry said, "We wrong both God and ourselves when our eye is more to men, the instruments of our crosses and comforts than to God the author."[4] Both Rachel and Leah had eyes looking more to each other than to God. The blessings of one sister became a cross for the other to bear. When our hearts are full of longing, we fresh-out-of-amazing girls often can't see blessings of others except as a cross to bear. We feel pierced by their prize. We bleed and we wonder why no one sees or cares.

But God, the Author, was not finished writing the story of loved and barren Rachel: "God *remembered* Rachel, and God *hearkened* to her, and opened her womb" (Genesis 30:22 KJV). Isn't that beautiful? *Hearken* is the Hebrew word *shama,* and it means "to hear with attention and understanding."[5] God had not abandoned Rachel even while he was working out the blessings he had for Leah. God had heard Rachel's prayers too. He understood her pain, and as he hearkened to her, he opened her womb and removed her shame. Rachel's manipulative ways could not end her own barrenness. Only God could. Yet from her limited perspective, she couldn't see that her efforts would be futile; she didn't let herself believe that God was at work.

A sister who walks with you and says, "I understand your hurt" is a blessing of great value.

Isn't that the case with us as well? We see only what we can see. God sees the bigger picture, and it is wide and deep and eternal. What did God see for Rachel? He saw her two sons being the focus of their father's affection. He saw one of her sons, Joseph, being hated by his brothers as a result of Jacob's faithfulness. But God also saw Joseph surviving a pit and a prison and then rising up to save his family from a famine. The Lord also saw Joseph declaring the goodness of an amazing God who works all things for our good and his glory.

I wonder what might have happened in this story if each sister had let her fresh-out-of-amazing heart connect with the other's instead of allowing comparison to destroy the relationship. How could Rachel and Leah have encouraged each other to trust God when it was hard to see him working? A sister who walks with you and says, "I understand your hurt" is a blessing of great value. She holds up weak arms and provides a safe place to be vulnerable. Of course we can't know what this would have meant for Leah and Rachel. But we can learn from their mistakes and live our lives differently in light of this truth. Oh, girls, there has to be a better way.

Imitation vs. Comparison

For years the Lord has been working on my heart regarding this matter of comparison. Lately, he has been whispering to me that being fresh out of amazing isn't a one-way ticket to despair; it is an opportunity to see God be big. When we see God as big, we lose the desire to merely look at the horizontal. It isn't that we completely miss all the things other amazing girls seem to be doing. But we aren't threatened by them because we are more aware of the work God is doing in us. In fact, we might even be drawn to imitate those same amazing girls.

Christ-controlled comparison can lead to imitating a life that pleases God. To live that way, we have to see others through God's eyes, and that requires we see him first. Understandably, we might need a little practice in that area.

Earlier this year my daughter Emma learned some hard lessons about making comparisons. Emma has been a dancer for eleven years. For much of that time, she was part of a ballet company that grew slowly. For years they held classes in a local church and did not have the traditional mirrors you see in most studio spaces. With only her instructor to guide her in her technique, Emma learned her steps and positions, eventually dancing on pointe. Much to the delight of the dancers this past year, the company was able to procure a new studio complete with hardwood floors and a wall of mirrors on two sides of the room.

Emma's joy in having a real studio was evident the first time I took her to class. Just before she went into the new studio, I said, "Have fun, but keep in mind you haven't been dancing in front of a mirror for years. I know it will be tempting to watch the other girls and compare yourself to them. Just keep your eyes on the instructor and on yourself more than on your friends." She smiled and went inside.

Within a few weeks I noticed a change in Emma's demeanor when I picked her up from dance. Where before she might have been tired after a rehearsal, my usually extroverted girl was now quiet and a bit withdrawn. Slowly, she had started questioning her own dance skills to the degree that she hinted at quitting altogether. I had an idea what might be going on, but it took several conversations to get to the heart of the matter. She admitted, "Mom, when I was dancing at the church, I only had my instructor in my view. She not only gave me correction, but she always offered me encouragement as well. I had nothing to compare myself to because she was the only one I could see. Now, since we have mirrors all around us as we dance, I'm watching the other girls too. They look different from me, and they dance differently. Now all I see is my own need for correction—and their confidence."

Later that week I happened to be talking to another dance mom whose daughter was feeling discouraged as well. She remarked, "Mirrors are great for instruction but horrible for comparison." When I relayed this to Emma, she seemed surprised that the other girls were feeling the exact same thing she was while they danced. In a moment of revelation and wisdom beyond her fifteen years, she said, "Mom, the mirror magnified my insecurities." And this understanding began to slow and eventually stop her downward spiral, and she resolved to keep dancing.

When we see God as big, we lose the desire to merely look at the horizontal. It isn't that we completely miss all the things other amazing girls seem to be doing. But we aren't threatened by them because we are more aware of the work God is doing in us.

In the end, what made the difference for my daughter was the truth found in Joshua 1:9: "Be strong and courageous. Do not be frightened, and do not be dismayed, for the LORD your God is with you wherever you go." The truth of God's presence in Emma's life set her free from the idea that she had to be a better version of what she saw in other girls. She didn't need to compare herself to the many. She only needed to imitate her instructor and strive to please the One who was with her and who would provide the courage she needed when she needed it most. She chose imitation over comparison, and this wise choice has served her well.

LOL at the Future

But what if you don't have imitation-worthy people in your life who will point you to Jesus? I know this might be a reality for you. I have gone through seasons in my life when I couldn't find a mentor or even a friend to grab coffee with on a regular basis. That's when I've been especially grateful that God has given us women in his Word we can imitate wholeheartedly. Consider the virtuous woman from Proverbs 31: "Strength and dignity are her clothing, and she laughs at the time to come."

Christ-controlled comparison can lead to
imitating a life that pleases God.

Like most of us reading this book, this woman is a follower of God. Like many of us, she is a wife and mom. And, perhaps like a few of us, she hears genuine and public praise from her people, she runs her household efficiently, she has a thriving clothing business as well, and she looks good while doing all this and more. But more importantly, she knows to clothe herself with God-given strength and dignity. She has no fear of the future because she fears God first. The sovereign and loving One she trusts holds the future, and she can smile in the face of it.

When God's love has the run of the house
of our hearts, there is no room for fear.

Based on this snapshot of her life, do you think this woman is struggling with the curse of comparison? It sure doesn't sound like it. Goodness, I want this to be true of me! Do you think a fresh-out-of-amazing girl can laugh at the future like the woman I just introduced? I believe she can.

Keep in mind, this book is about making progress. Sometimes we take baby steps, and other times we must make a leap of faith. Whatever the case may be, we have to get moving in the right direction and then keep moving. Since the curse of comparison in my own life has deep, deep roots, I wanted to have a solid plan in place for when, in my weak and weary moments, it raises its ugly head. This might just be the place to start so we too can LOL at the future:

L: Live Loved

The curse of comparison is fueled by our insecurity and our fear that we will never measure up to others. When we live rooted in the knowledge that we are loved unconditionally, the Bible tells us, our fear is driven away. The Message puts this truth in the most beautiful and heart-resonating way:

> God is love. When we take up permanent residence in a life of love, we live in God and God lives in us. This way, love has the run of the house, becomes at home and mature in us, so that we're free of worry on Judgment Day—our standing in the world is identical with Christ's. There is no room in love for fear. Well-formed love banishes fear. Since fear is crippling, a fearful life—fear of death, fear of judgment—is one not yet fully formed in love (1 John 4:17-18 MSG).

When God's love has the run of the house of our hearts, there is no room for fear. We are even set free to celebrate the good things God does in the lives of others because we are not afraid he is going to run out of blessings for us. How can God's "Never Stopping, Never Giving Up, Unbreaking, Always and Forever" love not cause us to laugh at the days to come?

Do you remember what Leah did when she knew she was loved in this way? Her life poured forth praise to God. Our lives can too, when our hearts are rooted in this kind of fear-banishing love.

O: Only One Member of the Audience Matters

So much of my fresh-out-of-amazing feelings arise because of the expectations I'm convinced others have for me. I think they need me to be amazing all the time. But, truthfully, that is hardly ever the case. Just because I feel the weight of people's expectations doesn't mean they actually have those—or any—expectations of me.

One thing I have found helpful to do when my heart is struggling in particular in this way is to reduce my audience to One. This involves two key steps:

Disengage: First I need to release myself from the expectations, real or perceived, I feel others have of me. Doing so might mean separating myself from the world's voices for a time. For me, that usually involves stepping away from the noise of social media and the daily chatter. One simple way for me to disengage is to listen to worshipful music and let the lyrics wash over my heart. This prepares me in the best way for the next step.

Engage: I need to get alone with God. I need to seek his heart. I need to tell him I am buried by my own perception that others have impossible expectations of me. Every time I do that, he releases my heart to please only One—himself. My daughter Emma said it like this: "All that I want to be, he already is. All that I want to do he has already done." Fixing my eyes on the author of my faith aligns my heart with his. I can rest in the work he has already done in my life. And I can show the world who he is instead of being bent under the weight of living in my own strength to show them who *I* am.

*Just because I feel the weight of people's
expectations doesn't mean they actually have
those—or any—expectations of me.*

L: Look to Connect, Not Compare

Connection trumps comparison any day. Why? Because connection helps us know we are not alone. Comparison makes us feel like we are the only one like us. Connection builds up our hearts; comparison either puffs us up with pride or tears us down in humiliation. Connection builds bridges; comparison digs holes. When we look to connect with other women instead of forming our opinions about them from a distance, we all benefit. And I have found the most powerful way to connect with another woman is to honestly share our broken places.

We don't have to impress in order to bless. We can open our hearts, share our fresh-out-of-amazing stories, and see God do a work only he can do. I mentioned this in *Hope for the Weary Mom: Let God Meet You in the Mess*: "Friends don't complete us. Friends complement us. Only God can fill our hearts with hope. True friends will point you to him." When we allow him to complete us first, we get the chance to be best supporting actress in another woman's God-given story. We have the affirmation of Scripture that God dwells in places where two or more gather in his name (Matthew 18:20). This place of connection becomes holy ground instead of a battleground because God joins you.

All that I want to be, God already is. All that
I want to do, he has already done.

Called Out. Called Up.

We have been called out of our cursed habit of comparison and called up to a higher place: to a community of connected hearts. That is what I experienced today. Timely, I know.

My friend Michal Lynn invited me to have brunch with her at a trendy local restaurant. We ate way too much down-home cooking, and I might have chased mine with an iced Nutella coffee or two. The coffee and the company were sweet.

In the middle of swapping stories, Michal Lynn called me out of hiding and up to community. It wasn't threatening. She just said, "Hey, would you consider something and pray about it?" No one had asked me to do that in quite a while. I was challenged in a good way, and her request endeared her to me instantly. You see, I'm learning that fresh-out-of-amazing girls do not have to walk alone. In fact, walking together encourages us greatly. Let's start today. Better yet, let's challenge other women to LOL at the future with us and call them out of the cursed habit of comparison as well.

Connection trumps comparison any day.

I truly believe that when we are fresh out of amazing, we deeply need the community we may be running from. So what one small step can you take to join hands with another sister in Christ so you can support each other? One idea might be to text a friend and say, "Are you fresh out of amazing? I'm reading a book by that title, and God is using it to stir up some stuff in my life and encourage me. Want to read along and meet me for coffee to discuss it?" After you finish this book, move on to a Bible study.

Whatever you decide to do, let's run the race set before us with perseverance, determined to fix our eyes on Jesus, and knowing that we are with others who are running the race as well. We can run it together and celebrate each other's hard-won victories.

Girls, this is the better way.

> **Interested in going deeper?** I created an LOL Mini-Challenge that you'll find on page 195. This is a seven-day challenge you can start today. It should only take a few minutes a day except for the final day. Who will you ask to join you?

Chapter 4

I Feel Like My Dreams Have Died

I arrived in the room early to get my heart as well as my presentation in order. God was certainly smiling on me because, right before my afternoon session, the conference I was attending pulled out a stunning coffee bar with delicious treats. I had two fast cups of coffee (don't judge) and a cupcake because who says no when God is clearly blessing you with snack love? Besides, this was the first time I was going to share my *Fresh Out of Amazing* story with other women, and I wasn't sure I was ready.

My nerves showed it. I was even less sure it would resonate with anyone else. To make matters worse, I didn't have anything left to give the women who might show up for my session at 4:00 p.m. on the final day of the conference. I had been wading in and out of being fresh out of amazing for the better part of six months, and a recent life-changing event had turned me into a weepy hot mess of a girl. I had cried three times at the conference when a few women asked precisely the right questions. What was I thinking stepping in front of a room full of women? I was thinking I needed this talk more than they did.

The conference theme was "Wild Obedience," and my act of wild obedience was moving forward with my session despite all my reservations. My friend Lisa-Jo Baker had said earlier at the conference, "Following Jesus is not about image management." Well, my image was lost about five minutes into my talk. I opened my heart for all to see because dreams that slip out of our grasp hurt that much. I thought I was going to share life-changing truth with them. Instead, on this day, I was the one deeply in need of Jesus, and everyone was watching. And I hadn't factored crying time into my talk!

The women sat quietly and were lovely about it all. Bless them, they cried too. Their tears gave me a little time to recover, I breathed a Jesus-help-me prayer, and he came running to strengthen me. He is all grace like that. I finished the talk and discovered once again that Jesus does beautiful work in our broken places. I felt like I had run a marathon in forty-five minutes. In many ways I had. But I hadn't run alone.

Some of the beauty of brokenness is found in God's tenderness toward us. Psalm 62:8 says, "Have faith in Him in all circumstances, *dear* people. Open up your heart to Him; the True God shelters us *in His arms*" (THE VOICE). When we open our heart to him, God shows up and shelters us. We are his daughters. His grace covers us at all times.

Hannah's Breaking

Hannah had a dream for years. It wasn't far-fetched or fancy. She didn't want riches or beauty. Hannah wanted something ordinary and everyday, something that many of us take for granted. The deepest longing of her heart was to be a mother.

> One day after they ate and drank at Shiloh, Hannah got up *and presented herself before the Lord.* It so happened that the priest Eli was sitting *in a place of honor* beside the doorpost of the Eternal's congregation tent *as Hannah entered.* She was heartbroken, and she began to pray to the Eternal One, weeping uncontrollably as she did (1 Samuel 1:9-10 THE VOICE).

Years and years of waiting had taken their toll, and Hannah found herself in a place where she didn't care at all about image management. She took her fresh-out-of-amazing self straight to God, and she cried bitter tears. Hannah bared her soul for all to see, overwhelmed by the feeling that her dreams had died. I am not sure we can fully understand the poverty of this moment and the depth of Hannah's lament.

Hannah's grief probably started out as soft weeping and quickly moved to a wailing that attracted the attention of Eli, the priest who was watching nearby. His response to her suggests the intensity of Hannah's emotions:

> How long are you going to continue drinking, *making a spectacle of yourself?* Stop drinking wine, *and sober up"*
> (1 Samuel 1:14 THE VOICE).

Hannah didn't have a sweet group of understanding women witnessing her brokenness before the Lord like I did at the conference. She had only a priest named Eli who accused her of being drunk, and he told her abruptly to quit causing a scene. Talk about being kicked when you're down! But this was not the first time Hannah was misunderstood or treated poorly. This would be a great place to pause and take note of how a fresh-out-of-amazing girl is often treated by those around her. I think the main reason is because our brokenness tends to make some people feel uncomfortable. Maybe you can relate to what was happening in Hannah's life.

Hannah's Husband

Hannah was married to Elkanah, and she was one of his two wives. The reason he had two wives may have had something to do with Hannah. Her barrenness might have persuaded him to take another. In spite of his less-than-perfect matrimonial status, Elkanah was faithful to the Lord and went every year to worship and offer sacrifices to God. He would share a portion of his offering with Peninnah, his other wife, and her children. Then, even though God had not given her children, Elkanah gave to Hannah a double portion of the sacrificed meat.

Elkanah loved Hannah dearly, but he didn't quite understand her desperation. She wept. She refused to eat. "Hannah," he would say, "isn't my love better than your having a whole lot of sons? Don't be sad." I'm not going to take shots at Elkanah for being a clueless husband, but perhaps he might have had a better way of trying to console his heartbroken wife. But the truth is, friends, only God knows the depth of the pain in our fresh-out-of-amazing hearts. It would have been awesome if Hannah's man had gotten it too. I would have liked for him to hold her and cry with her. Many men do that for their wives. But often, when we are just plain broken, God doesn't want us to settle for the understanding that our husbands and our dear friends can offer. He wants us to go to him.

Hannah's Bully

So Hannah had a husband who loved her but could not understand her desperate longing for a child. Her barrenness and her not being understood by Elkanah would have been burden enough, but Hannah was dealing with more. She lived with a bully who was in full attack mode:

> Peninnah used to infuriate Hannah until Hannah trembled with irritation because the Eternal had not given Hannah children. This went on year after year; and every time Hannah went up to the house of the Eternal, Peninnah would infuriate her (1 Samuel 1:6-7 THE VOICE).

Hannah's adversary was vexing and her insults, chafing. Hearing Peninnah's words was like having salt rubbed into an open wound.

Peninnah was working herself into a more powerful position by demeaning Hannah, taunting her about her childlessness, and mocking her near-dead dream. Sweet Hannah, we understand. We have an enemy too. Only his name is not Peninnah. His name is Satan, and he likes to rub salt in our wounds. As we learned in the previous chapter, when we are fresh out of amazing, Satan often parades people in front of us whose dreams have not died, whose dreams may even have been realized beyond anyone's expectations. And, friends, Satan gets great delight in tormenting us like that.

These might have seemed like daunting obstacles for Hannah to face, but in reality, they were opportunities for God to minister his grace to her. Every bit of comfort in Hannah's life had been removed. My friend Lara shared these facts about eagles that support the important role that a *lack* of comfort can play:

> Before a baby eagle learns to fly, her mother makes the nest extremely uncomfortable. She removes all the soft parts that make it cozy and warm. Essentially she is creating a place the eaglet no longer wants to stay. She wants her baby to fly and soar to heights she can't imagine and staying in the nest won't allow her to do so.[1]

Could it be that God was inviting Hannah to fly to him instead of to the comfort of her husband? Could Hannah's soul have finally reached a breaking point because of Peninnah's torment? Hannah was flying now. She was flying straight to the heart of God, and she could not have imagined where it would take her.

Hannah's Prayer

"Childless, Hannah was not prayerless. Barren, she still believed, and her pain found a refuge in prayer."[2]

Hannah fled to that refuge. She knew about persisting in prayer. In 1 Samuel 1, hers is not the casual prayer of a woman who does not know her God:

> [Hannah] was deeply distressed and prayed to the LORD and wept bitterly. And she vowed a vow and said, "O

Lord of hosts, if you will indeed look on the affliction of your servant and remember me and not forget your servant, but will give to your servant a son, then I will give him to the Lord all the days of his life, and no razor shall touch his head."

As she continued praying before the Lord, Eli observed her mouth. Hannah was speaking in her heart; only her lips moved, and her voice was not heard (1 Samuel 1:10-13).

Years of asking and waiting had produced in Hannah an unbearable heavy heartedness, but she was not angry. Hannah was broken, not bitter. The tears of agony and the desperate prayers she poured out to the Lord were precious to him. He who collects every one of our tears in a bottle was listening (see Psalm 56:8). Hannah knew the power of prayer. Psalm 62:5-8 reminds me of Hannah:

> For God alone, O my soul, wait in silence,
>   for my hope is from him.
> He only is my rock and my salvation,
>   my fortress; I shall not be shaken.
> On God rests my salvation and my glory;
>   my mighty rock, my refuge is God.
> Trust in him at all times, O people;
>   pour out your heart before him;
>   God is a refuge for us.

Hannah's faith was fueled by her fiery belief that she could trust God at all times and for everything. She poured out her heart to her rock and her salvation. In doing so, she quieted the voices of those around her and fine-tuned her heart to listen for his answer.

Jesus does beautiful work in our broken places.

Friends, this might be a good place to simply put down your book and ask yourself a few questions. There is so much more to Hannah's story, but we can't miss this moment.

- Are you barren yet still believing?
- Have you found refuge in prayer?
- Will you quiet the voices around you and focus on God's still small voice?
- Is God your hope? Your salvation? Your glory?

Maybe you are struggling at this point and having a crisis of belief. I want you to know you are not the only one who feels this way.

My friend Emily felt her dreams had died when her husband of two years shared with her that God was calling him into full-time pastoral ministry. Emily didn't feel joy. She didn't feel proud of her husband. She was mad at him and God because this wasn't the life she'd signed up for.

One day she was sitting in Bible study listening to all the other women talk about how they loved God, and they meant every word they spoke. Emily couldn't take it anymore. She excused herself to the bathroom and had what she called a mini nervous breakdown. When she came back to the group, the pastor's wife asked, "Emily, are you okay?"

With that, Emily told me, "I lost it. Lost it big! Ugly cry, word vomit lost it. And they all ran to me—like sweet friends do—even though in my heart I'd always believed they thought I was too rough around the edges."

Suzanne, the pastor's wife, asked Emily a second question that stunned her: "Do you think maybe you're mad at God?" Suzanne continued, "If so, don't you think you should tell him about it? You have got to get past this, and you won't be able to if you're not honest with God."

Emily wondered why in the world she would tell God she was mad at him. The idea was just plain awful. How could she do that? Deep down in her too-rough-around-the-edges heart, she wondered if God saw her angry heart and cared about her anyway. But with nothing left to lose at this point, Emily decided to give it a try. She took off work one afternoon, went home to her tiny, lonely house, and threw a two-hour temper tantrum at the feet of Jesus. "I believe with my whole heart that he was so sad for my pain and so glad that I was finally telling him about it! Afterward, I apologized and acknowledged that I couldn't possibly understand his ways because they are infinitely better than mine."

Oh, Lord, deal with our fresh-out-of-amazing
hearts. We may be barren right now, but stir in
our hearts a vibrant and living faith in you.

From that day forward, Emily's heart began to slowly soften, heal, and believe again. Something shifted that day as she laid her broken heart before the Lord. In doing so, she communicated to him her trust. I love how Emily closed her story: "When we shout our ache while clinging to his robe, we actually build our relationship with him. It is his sweet upside-down way."

When we are fresh out of amazing, we need to remember God's great faithfulness. Just like Emily did, we may need to shout our ache to Jesus while clinging to his robe. We need to be certain in our heart of hearts that God is good and that he is working out a good plan we can't yet see. We need to be sure that he has not left us alone and then rest in that knowledge. This is a critical part of our journey, and I think without a doubt Hannah was convinced of it.

God Breaks Through

I don't know why God chose this moment to remember Hannah and move on her behalf. Clearly, he was working according to a plan Hannah could not see. In answering her prayer, he put into motion a story that would include not only her son, but empires, kings, and ultimately a Savior for the whole world. The truth stands: often our breaking point births a bigger story. From her perspective Hannah couldn't imagine a bigger story, and for that matter, rarely do we.

Remember, of course, Hannah still had to respond to Eli and his accusation that she was drunk in the house of God. I love that Hannah didn't react. She spoke respectfully to Eli:

> "No, my lord, I am a woman troubled in spirit. I have drunk neither wine nor strong drink, but I have been pouring out my soul before the LORD. Do not regard your servant as a worthless woman, for all along I have been speaking out of my great anxiety and vexation." Then Eli answered, "Go in peace, and the God of Israel grant your petition that you have made to him." And she said, "Let your servant find favor in your eyes." Then the woman went her way and ate, and her face was no longer sad (1 Samuel 1:15-18).

As if a mighty rushing wind of grace had blown through the air, Hannah's sadness lifted. God had heard her cry, and a few months later she held in her arms an answered prayer she named Samuel. In the years she was empty and waiting, God was developing in her the character of a mother who would march right back to the temple three years later and make good on her vow.

God does not waste our fresh-out-of-amazing years, my friend. If we allow him, he uses that season of our life to refine us and prepare us for the greater works he will call us to down the road.

Often our breaking point births a bigger story.

Hannah allowed God to mold her and make her into a woman who could not help but bless the Lord even as she offered back the one gift her heart had yearned for most. She was now giving back to God as an offering of praise and thanksgiving the dream she thought had died. She expressed her thoughts and feelings in the most beautiful way.

> My heart exults in the LORD;
>> my horn is exalted in the LORD.
> My mouth derides my enemies,
>> because I rejoice in your salvation.
> There is none holy like the LORD:
>> for there is none besides you;
>> there is no rock like our God (1 Samuel 2:1-2).

Thousands of years later and inspired by the Holy Spirit, another mother—this one named Mary—would echo the song of Hannah in her own *Magnificat*:

> My soul magnifies the Lord,
>> and my spirit rejoices in God my Savior,
> for he has looked on the humble estate of his servant.
>> For behold, from now on all generations will
>> call me blessed;

for he who is mighty has done great things for me,
and holy is his name (Luke 1:46-49).

Hannah had no idea that her faith would inspire and be imitated by the mother of Jesus. I find this part of the story absolutely breathtaking. Hannah and Mary, two mothers separated by generations, both offered their miracle sons back to God to serve him. Hannah and Mary both came to understand on a deep level that God uses everything in our lives for our good and his glory. And sometimes he does so in the most amazing ways—especially when we are out of amazing ourselves.

> God does not waste our fresh-out-of-amazing years. If we allow him, he uses that season of our life to refine us and prepare us for the greater works he will call us to down the road.

If you keep reading the book of 1 Samuel, you will learn that year after year Hannah visited her son Samuel in the temple and took him a handmade robe to wear. It was her way of reminding him that she loved him. I imagine she prayed over every stitch she sewed and asked God to bless her son. Scripture tells us that "the boy Samuel grew in the presence of the Lord" (1 Samuel 2:21). And God further blessed Hannah by giving her three more sons and two daughters. What a sweet ending!

My dear friend, I'm learning there is great hope beyond the place of being fresh out of amazing. Author Jon Bloom said, "The promises of God believed produce the energy of hope."[3] What if, when we feel like our dreams have died, we believed God's promise found in Isaiah 58?

The Lord will guide you continually
and satisfy your desire in scorched places
and make your bones strong;
and you shall be like a watered garden,
like a spring of water,
whose waters do not fail.
And your ancient ruins shall be rebuilt;
you shall raise up the foundations of many generations;
you shall be called the repairer of the breach,
the restorer of streets to dwell in (verses 11-12).

Like Hannah, we can trust that God will satisfy our desires in our own scorched place. We can pour out our hearts to him even when they are filled with anger and pain. Hannah watched as God rebuilt the ruins of her life and laid a foundation for many generations to come. God will be faithful to us too. Instead of leaving us with a pile of dead dreams, God will make hope rise again in our hearts.

Chapter 5

Liar, Liar, Pants on Fire

Sometimes when I read fairy tales to my girls, I find between the lines a more powerful lesson for my own heart than they hear in the actual story. Those moments remind me that God is certainly not limited in my life when he wants to speak truth to my heart. He can use everything and anything to get my attention, and I think twentieth-century writer, poet, and theologian G.K. Chesterton would agree. I am guessing that he might have had more than just children in mind when he wrote this:

> Fairy tales...are not responsible for producing in children fear, or any of the shapes of fear; fairy tales do not give the child the idea of the evil or the ugly; that is in the child already, because it is in the world already. Fairy tales do not give the child his first idea of bogey. What fairy tales give the child is his first clear idea of the possible defeat of bogey. The baby has known the dragon intimately ever since he had an imagination. What the fairy tale provides for him is a St. George to kill the dragon. Exactly what the fairy tale does is this: it accustoms him for a series of clear pictures to the idea that these limitless terrors had a limit, that these shapeless enemies have

enemies in the knights of God, that there is something in the universe more mystical than darkness, and stronger than strong fear.[1]

As I was thinking about this chapter and feeling inspired by Chesterton's point, I decided to make up a fairy tale for us too. By the way, my girls loved it. I think it might be their favorite thing I have ever written:

Once upon a time there was a fair maiden who lived accidentally in a land called Fresh Out of Amazing. I say accidentally *because her true home was called the Land of the Rising Sun. It was joyful and filled with hope because the King, her Father, ruled the land with truth and honor.*

But one day, curious about the land just beyond her kingdom, the fair maiden wandered far from her home. And that was when she came across an evil dragon named Liar Liar. At first he flattered her and promised her all things good and glamorous, the very things her father had warned her might cause a root of pride to grow therein. Liar Liar soon found a way to her heart. Once that was done, he easily took her to a broken-down castle made of lies and held her captive.

Every night he would swoop down and breathe blazing hot threats of horribleness to the fair maiden. He would tell her she was ugly, forgotten, and alone, and he would make her wonder how—or even if— anyone could ever love her. After a while, the dragon didn't need to keep the doors and windows locked to keep her inside. She stayed willingly because she believed Liar Liar, and she allowed the fear his words caused to hold her inside. The fair maiden let fear keep her from being brave and returning to the Land of the Rising Sun, the land of freedom and her Father's love, the land that had been home.

So there in the land of Fresh Out of Amazing, she hid, forgetting who she was, how much her Father loved her, and the freedom that would come if she returned home.

Well, perhaps like you, I've met more than a few lying dragons in my life. In *Hope for the Weary Mom,* I wrote, "Lies are slick, often wrapped in a small element of truth, and connected to other basic lies we are prone to believe. The challenge we face is untangling the mess."[2] This tangled-up mess sounds a lot like the land of Fresh Out of Amazing in our story, doesn't it? I need to be reminded regularly that lying dragons can be killed, they need to be killed, and there is only one way to do it.

How to Kill a Lying Dragon

The dragons we meet in real life can be just as frightening as the ones that lived under our beds when we were five years old. And just as the King's daughter in my fairy tale experienced, dragons of the lying kind can certainly keep us locked in a land that seems hopeless and dark. But we are not children of the dark; we are "daughters of the day. We are not created of night or owned by darkness" (1 Thessalonians 5:5 THE VOICE). The trouble is, the dark places can hold us captive. Good thing for us, the Master Dragon Slayer is willing to meet us in those dark places and carry us safely home.

Watching the Master at Work

In John 4 we meet a maiden not so unlike us. She is living in a land steeped in history called Samaria. Matthew Henry said, "Here lay Jacob's ground, the parcel of ground which Jacob gave to his son Joseph whose bones were buried in it."[3] But since the days of the patriarchs, Samaria had been a valley of trouble mixed with a people of complicated heritage. They were part Jewish, yet hated by the Jews—and the feelings were mutual. In fact, the Jews had absolutely no dealings with the Samaritans.

We understand, don't we? Maybe you know from your own experience that a complicated heritage can cause lies to dwell and reproduce. The lies are our "normal," and we go about life as usual. Until one day a doorway called Hope opens to our hearts, and we see there is a better way to live. That's what we see in this account of the woman at the well.

As Bible teacher Beth Moore says, when you take down a lie, you must replace it with a truth. Consider these four truths that play out in John 4 as the Samaritan woman and Jesus talk. Each of these truths displaces a common lie we women are prone to believe. Let's watch and learn as Jesus slays the woman's dragons—and ours— one by one.

> **Lie 1:** Jesus doesn't know what is happening in my life.
>
> **Truth 1:** Jesus comes to us and walks with us through whatever is happening in our lives.

If you don't read the beginning of John 4, you will miss a key point. I confess, sometimes as I read my Bible, I'm tempted to skip over geography and big names I can't pronounce. But in the first few sentences of John 4, we learn a precious truth that is central to taking down our first lie:

> When Jesus learned that the Pharisees had heard that Jesus was making and baptizing more disciples than John (although Jesus himself did not baptize, but only his disciples), he left Judea and departed again for Galilee. And he had to pass through Samaria (John 4:1-4).

What do you think of when you read the words "he had to pass through Samaria"? I think to myself, *This must have been the only route for Jesus to take to get from point A (Judea) to point B (Galilee).* But did he have to pass through Samaria? No. He could have walked along the coast of the Mediterranean Sea west of Samaria or along the River Jordan on the eastern side. For years Jews had been walking around the land of Samaria. They avoided this area. Simply put, for traveling purposes Jesus did not have to pass through Samaria. But he did. Why?

I believe it was because his Father had planned for him a divine appointment with a woman who needed to know God saw her. God was keenly aware of her desperate situation. He knew she was buried in lies and being held captive by her fears and the life she was living. He also knew that she was not seeking his heart this day, but he was most definitely seeking hers.

Jesus knows what is happening in our lives. He seeks us. He comes to us and does not leave us the same.

Consider the perspective Elisabeth Elliot offers: "In every event He seeks an entrance to my heart, yes, even in my most helpless, futile, fruitless moments. The very cracks and empty crannies of my life, my perplexities and hurts and botched-up jobs, He wants to fill with Himself, His joy, His life."[4] Going to the well may have felt like an unremarkable moment for the Samaritan woman. Maybe she was thinking about her botched-up life as she walked along. Or maybe she felt lost or alone, sure that nobody—especially God— cared about her. I know I struggle quite a bit with the lie that God doesn't know what is happening in my life, and this lie quickly spirals out of control, enticing me to sin and despair. I can tell you from experience, this path never leads to good things.

Yet in this story of the Samaritan and Jesus at the well, I see with my own eyes that Jesus comes after us. He doesn't leave us alone in the dark to find our own way. This scene offers a beautiful illustration of this truth that Jesus himself spoke: "The Son of Man came to seek and to save the lost" (Luke 19:10). When we are fresh out of amazing, we have to believe with all our hearts that Jesus knows what is happening in our lives and that he will come to wherever we are—whether Samaria, San Francisco, or Starbucks. Jesus is always seeking a way to our heart. So, girls, let's slay the Dragon of Lie 1 right now with the soul-settling truth: Jesus knows what is happening in our lives. He seeks us. He comes to us and does not leave us the same.

Lie 2: My mess is too much for Jesus.

Truth 2: Nothing is impossible for Jesus.

I sometimes wonder if people who read all my weary-mom writings and musings might get their fill, if they haven't already. Some of these gals may have cast me off and thought, "Girlfriend, you need to put the veil back on and tell me life is fine." No can do.

And like these readers I may lose, I'm sure you have had people disappear from your life at precisely the moment your world fell apart. Often people just can't deal with our mess because they have messes too. I get it. Sometimes my mess just feels too much even for me to handle. Similarly, when I'm fresh out of amazing, I might also be the one to avoid people who are hurting. I hide, I skip opportunities to bump into friends at church, and I don't return phone calls because I just can't even say the words to one more person. My frayed-around-the-edges life is almost too much to bear and definitely too much to share.

The Samaritan woman was hiding in the middle of her life too. Scripture tells us it was about the sixth hour of the day when she went to draw water. The other women would have come and gone from the well hours before because the sixth hour was noon, the hottest part of the day. She chose to come to the well to get her water during the hottest and loneliest part of the day because she wanted to avoid the stares of the other women. She wanted to be alone—but on this day she wasn't. She encountered Jesus. What's more, he spoke to her and made a request: "Give me a drink" (John 4:7).

I can picture her spinning around and barking, "You talkin' to me?" She didn't exactly respond with grace. Truthfully, when I am fresh out of amazing, my first response to the needs of others is not usually grace and a smile either. And in her defense, she rightly acknowledged that Jesus was a Jew and she was a Samaritan. And then there was the tiny little fact that he, a man, was speaking to a woman in public. This was not a normal interaction by any means.

What choice did Jesus have here? He could have said, "Oh, you're right. You and I shouldn't be talking—and clearly you aren't in any mood to serve me water or chat. I'll move on." Jesus could have cast her off for several good reasons: his rank as Son of God, her lowly position of a poor Samaritan woman, and her terse response, to name a few. But he did not do any such thing. "Though she spoke perversely, Christ did not cast her off, but instructed and encouraged her," says Matthew Henry.[5] Jesus stayed. He instructed her. He encouraged her broken heart, and he made her a life-changing offer.

I am writing this right now with tears in my eyes because, girls, on far too many days I am just flat-out mean to my people. I'm even meaner to God when he says, "Give me a minute of your day." My heart hardens as the enemy whispers to me, "You know your messy life is too much for others. For goodness' sake, it's too much for you. Of course it is way too much for God." That lying dragon says it over and over, and I am tempted to crumble completely under the barrage. But Jesus is not sitting across the table from you or me saying that the situation is beyond his paygrade. He is leaning in close and looking into our eyes, and saying, "I will not cast you off, sweet girl. Not ever."

Lie 3: Jesus isn't enough for me.

Truth 3: Jesus offers precisely what we need.

Isn't it interesting how the lies we believe mix themselves all up together and feed off one another? It reminds me of my girls' knitting projects. My daughters—who range in age from six to six-teen—decided to spend this summer sitting in a knitting circle and watching the Harry Potter movies. Knit one, purl two, knit one, purl two—it goes on over and over again—until they hit a snag. You see, my girls aren't always careful about their ball of yarn tagging along behind their knitting. I find unwound yarn balls wrapped around the leg of a coffee table, trailing into the dining room, and heading up the stairs.

I have cautioned them over and over again to keep their yarn in order or else they will find themselves in a pretty unfortunate mess. I suppose I could sit and wrap up their yarn balls, but I find it a bet-ter life lesson to let them experience the consequences themselves. My mom is a far more patient friend to my girls. A couple of years ago, she sat for at least two hours working on a knot of epic propor-tions because the yarn was someone's favorite color. The knot was massive and entangled with other smaller knots. At one point my mom gave up, and my dad finished the task. Of course he smiled, untangled it, and thanked her for getting the worst of it worked out so he could be the hero. (I don't think she really minded one bit.)

Our life messes are not too different from knotted yarn. The lies we believe are often tangled around one another. In fact, if you think about it, a lie is actually fertile ground for another to grow. As lies spawn other lies, they knot themselves up right in the middle of our lives and we are forced to sit and untangle the mess. If we don't, we will not be much good to anyone.

Jesus is not sitting across the table from you or me saying that the situation is beyond his paygrade. He is leaning in close and looking into our eyes, and saying, "I will not cast you off, sweet girl. Not ever."

Think with me about the two lies we have discussed so far and watch what the progression suggests about the next lie on our list. If the lying dragon we face can convince us that God doesn't know what is happening in our lives, then he can most certainly wrap us up in a mess that leads us to further believe our mess is too much for God to handle. If our mess is too much for the Lord, the logical response is to take matters into our own hands. Sure we need God, but we need something else too. The lie becomes greater as we slip into believing that we are too much for him and that he is not enough for us. Believing the lie is like tugging on one end of the yarn, and we make matters worse. What or who can counter our tendency to believe those lies?

We need a patient friend to come along and show us where to start unraveling the mess we have made. Jesus is that patient friend. He is able to speak directly to the heart of our deepest need. In fact, he did exactly that for the Samaritan woman when he said this:

> You don't know the gift of God or who is asking you for
> a drink *of this water from Jacob's well.* Because if you did,
> you would have asked Him *for something greater;* and He
> would have given you the living water (John 4:10 THE
> VOICE).

The woman had come that day to fill her pitcher, but Jesus offered her something greater. He knew that her spiritual thirst far exceeded the physical. He wants to give her something that would fill her thirsty soul. But in the heat of the day, in the middle of an unexpected conversation with Jesus, she almost missed it.

> The woman said to him, "Sir, you have nothing to draw
> water with, and the well is deep. Where do you get that
> living water?" (John 4:11)

Jesus offered this fresh-out-of-amazing girl living water, and all she could think of was the practical matter of how he was going to get it. She was more interested in the *where* and the *how* than the *what* Jesus was offering.

Before we get all judgmental, know that we do the same thing. Often we don't see the truth that's right in front of us. We can miss it once, twice, three times, or more. Lucky for us—and for this Samaritan woman—Jesus is not deterred from his mission. He went on to explain to the woman that even this well of Jacob she wanted to draw water from will never truly satisfy. But, he said, "I offer water that will become a wellspring within you that gives life throughout eternity. You will never be thirsty again" (John 4:14 THE VOICE).

Once again, he gently turned her gaze from that which she could see to the eternal where her heart will become a wellspring of living water. Something *greater.* Something *living is here.* Surely she will respond? Wouldn't we?

If we want streams of living water to flow into us, we have to believe Jesus is enough. We don't need him and something else. Nor do we need to know the how or the why. We simply need to receive and drink deeply of the grace-filled living water only Jesus offers.

"*Please*, Sir, give me some of this water, so I'll never be thirsty," she pleaded. Finally! Yes, she got it! But then she added, "And never again have to make the trip to this well" (verse 15 THE VOICE). The Samaritan woman had been coming to this well for so long all she could think about was never making the trip again. *Just fix me*, she was saying. *Give it to me. Give me what I need.* She wasn't really asking for the living water; she was asking for relief from her fresh-out-of-amazing life. She was still trapped in the thinking that a thing or a person could fix her problem. Maybe she thought that having a man could fix all her problems. For us, the fix-all might be a house, a job, or kids who behave at Target. "Lord, give me that. Give me that answer to my first-world problems, and I will be fine. I need *that*, Lord. Give it to me. Now."

But that, my friend, is the lie we are trapped into thinking. The truth is, Jesus is enough. Our life hidden with him in God is the enough we need. If we want streams of living water to flow in, we have to believe Jesus is enough. We don't need him and something else. Nor do we need to know the how and the why. We simply need to receive and drink deeply of the grace-filled living water only Jesus offers.

> **Lie 4:** Jesus will condemn me.
>
> **Truth 4:** Jesus only tells us the truth—
> and he speaks it with love.

"I die of thirst beside the fountain," wrote a poet.[6] Is it possible to be standing beside the wellspring of living water, dying of thirst but blind to the gift? It is, and she was. The Samaritan woman's sin had created a deep well in her soul, and she was drowning. Maybe in her heart she wanted a sip from the wellspring, but every time she tried to say so, shame pushed her back down. *Surely*, she undoubtedly thought, *the Rabbi would walk away if he knew who I am, what I am.*

Of course Jesus already knew because nothing is hidden from his sight. He saw her struggling and, like shooting an arrow straight into the bull's-eye, he spoke: "Go, call your husband, and come here." I wonder if she averted her eyes when she answered him flatly, "I have no husband."

Truth drew her. Truth revealed her to
herself. Truth set her free.

Jesus's response was truthful yet completely free of condemnation. Jesus agreed with her that she technically had no husband. He
knew she had had five of them, and the man she lived with was not
one of them. Jesus exposed her wound to bring healing; he did not
beat her down. This is what Matthew Henry said:

> In short, *she lived in adultery*. Yet observe how mildly
> Christ tells her of it; he doth not call her *strumpet*, but
> tells her, *He with whom thou livest is not thy husband*:
> and then leaves it to her own conscience to say the rest.
> Note, Reproofs are ordinarily *most profitable* when they
> are *least provoking*.[7]

By the standards of her day, this woman was a prostitute or, at
the very least, a promiscuous woman. Jesus didn't use those words,
but neither did he ignore the fact that they were accurate. Truth
spoken in love draws a heart out into the open, and that is precisely
what Jesus did.

Jesus and the woman went on to discuss many things, including
where the proper place to worship might be and the Messiah she
heard might be coming. His words must have cut like a knife: "The
Anointed is speaking to you. I am the One you have been looking
for" (THE VOICE).

Can you imagine what she must have felt? She had been search-
ing for him her whole life. She tried to find love and acceptance in
every man who would have her. Today, fresh out of amazing and
in the middle of her mundane dried-up life, she was looking at the

long-awaited One. He was standing right in front of her. I can't even comprehend it, friends. "The One you have been looking for" must have echoed in her ears until—and even long after—her heart grabbed hold of it. Truth drew her. Truth revealed her. Truth set her free.

In fact, truth set this woman so free that she ran back to town and told the same people she'd been hiding from to "Come and see this man." She who had hidden from people in the middle of the day was now testifying about Jesus all over town. Scripture tells us many believed and started their own faith journey that day: "The Samaritans approached Jesus and repeatedly invited Him to stay with them, so He lingered there for two days *on their account*" (verse 40 THE VOICE).

I love that Jesus lingered. Jesus wasn't in a hurry, though I'm sure the disciples were trying to move him on to the next town. Jesus gave two whole days to this group of people who were lost, broken, sinful, and fresh out of amazing. Jesus lingered and poured out living water because that is just what beautiful, amazing, truth-telling Jesus does. He lingers with the broken.

For the Days Those Lying Dragons Come Back Around

Watching Jesus kill the dragons swarming around the Samaritan woman teaches us that lying dragons can indeed be killed. Jesus slayed them one by one with truth. But if we neglect to prepare for their attack, we will be just like our fair maiden at the beginning of this chapter who had every power to leave her captive's lair, but no resolve to do so. When we resolve ahead of time to slay the lying dragons, the land of Fresh Out of Amazing will not be our permanent home. So, how do we prepare? It is as easy as ABC:

Acknowledge that you are prone to believing lies. The enemy wouldn't use lies as a strategy to render us ineffective if it didn't work. And look at what I read recently: "As fallen women, we are particularly prone to fall prey to Satan's deception. Remember that he did not first approach the man; he deliberately approached and deceived the woman...Satan targets women for deception."[8] We also know that "pride goes before destruction" (Proverbs 16:18). Do not pridefully think for one minute that you won't be a target of the enemy and that he doesn't have a sack full of lies he wants you to believe. In fact, his target is so specific he has a sack with your name on it.

Be aware of the lies you believe: You can start with the four lies I mentioned in this chapter. I think they are common to most women. However, given a few minutes, your Bible, and a piece of paper, you should be able to identify any other lies you struggle with. Maybe you need to make a pot of coffee, invite a friend over, and work through this exercise together. You might even be able to help each other identify lies you're believing. Do not stop until you have a sense that, at least right now, your list includes all the lies that entangle you. Be sure to mark in red the lie you think is the trigger for all the others. Remember mine? "God doesn't know what is happening to me." If I buy that one, I'm a goner.

Charge back with truth: For every lie you write down, list a truth from Scripture that charges back. This is the most important part of the plan. Don't be afraid to speak these truths aloud on the tough days. Write them on note cards, put them on your bathroom mirror, lay one next to the kitchen sink, and put another in the car. Think of these as hand grenades of truth that will "[demolish] arguments and ideas, every high-and-mighty philosophy that pits itself against the knowledge of the one true God" (2 Corinthians 10:5 THE VOICE). And so it is with every thought. Every emotion. Every lie. We take them captive to obey Christ. When we do this, they have no chance.

Jesus lingered and poured out living water because
that is just what beautiful, amazing, truth-telling
Jesus does. He lingers with the broken.

Meanwhile, somewhere in the Land of the Rising Sun...

The fair maiden remained a fearful captive until one day she remembered what her Father had told her long ago: a daughter of the true king has nothing to fear. No lie can hold her captive because the truth has already set her free. He had sung a song over her that found her once again.

Daughter.

Chosen.

Heiress.

Loved.

Suddenly, she called out to him with her whole heart, and he was there even as the words escaped her mouth. Abba, Daddy, came to her. She knew without a doubt she was safe. She always was when she was mindful of his loving presence. He caught her up in the strongest embrace and carried her home where she belonged. The Land of the Rising Sun was gleaming, just as she remembered it.

Chapter 6

When You've Lost Your Song in the Valley of Bitterness

I will allure her, and bring her into the wilderness, and speak comfortably unto her. And I will give her vineyards from thence, and the valley of Achor for a door of hope: and she shall sing there, as in the days of her youth, and as in the day when she came up out of the land of Egypt.

HOSEA 2:14-15 KJV

*I*f there were a chapter I wish I could skip out on writing, this is the one. I know with all my heart one reason we find ourselves fresh out of amazing is loss and grief. I've watched many friends walk the valley of Achor (the name means *bitterness*) and felt helpless. I had no clue how to respond except to pray, and I've prayed desperate prayers in the wee hours of the morning on behalf of hurting friends. But until a year ago, I hadn't experienced this valley personally. I didn't know its landscape or understand the waves of emotion I would encounter there. All that changed with a single phone call. The valley of Achor became my spiritual and emotional home for months when I experienced the soul-shattering loss of someone I loved dearly.

In the weeks leading up to the day of the phone call, I was already on edge. Life had been crazy full with writing, traveling, my husband being out of the country, speaking engagements, teaching, and chauffeuring my girls to extracurricular activities. Burdened and busy in every way possible, I was struggling to find an inch of margin where I could take a deep breath. Looking back, I also see signs along the way that God was trying to get my attention. He wanted to speak words of hope and encouragement to my heart, but with so much going on, I really didn't have much time to hear him. I was living what C.S. Lewis noted:

> We can ignore even pleasure. But pain insists upon being attended to. God whispers to us in our pleasures, speaks in our conscience, but shouts in our pains: it is his megaphone to rouse a deaf world.[1]

Can I tell you a secret? God always has a large megaphone with our name on it because the work he wants to do in our lives is necessary to make us more like Christ. God loves us enough to allow us to spend time in the valley of Achor. He knows that, during our walk in the wilderness, *fresh out of amazing* takes on a whole new meaning. And he is there.

It was cooler than normal for March. My husband was about to head out the door for work when he asked if I needed the van for the day. I told him I was planning to take the girls shopping for bathing suits with hopes of making it to the beach before the week was out. Wishing me good luck, he happily headed for work on his motorcycle, and I finished my third cup of coffee.

I let the girls sleep in because, for goodness' sake, it was spring break. My house was recovering from the buzz of activity over the past few weeks, and I was looking over my to-do list. I had one tiny e-mail to write and a short video to send to (in)courage for their upcoming online conference called (in)Real Life. They were featuring my faithful group of college friends from Indiana University. My daughter Abby was out of bed by now and she agreed to be my videographer. Around here, if you are available, you might be employed and paid in powdered sugar donuts, which were also flowing that day because, yes, it was spring break. The other girls woke up one by one, and I told them to get dressed because we were going shopping. Do you know what an announcement like this does to a house full of girls? Imagine feeding time at the zoo. You could say they were a bit excited, and that would be an understatement. They were dressed and waiting downstairs by the door in record time. If only they had the same reaction when I asked them to unload the dishwasher, life would be close to perfect.

I hit send on my e-mail and saw that my phone was ringing. I say *saw* because my phone was still on silent from the night before. It was a small miracle that I saw it ring. I recognized my mom's number and of course answered immediately. Admittedly, I was a bit surprised because we had spoken the day before for well over an hour. I had told her all about my trip to New York for a conference the previous week where Brooke and I had spoken on the topic of "How to Have Hope *Now*." She was a proud mom and had added, as usual, that she had no idea how I write and speak. "You must get that from your dad," she'd said, and then went on to tell me he had had a pretty good weekend and now was at his third and final radiation treatment. My dad had heroically battled cancer on and off for five years.

A few weeks before this spring break phone call, my dad had been diagnosed with a brain tumor and had started undergoing treatment. "Can you believe he went to the golf course?" Mom said. I smiled, knowing that was his happy place. I told her we thought of driving up to Indiana for the rest of the week, but she said resolutely not to come. "Your dad starts chemo on Wednesday, and he will not feel well. It would be better for you to come later when school is out. It will be summer, and he will feel so much better then. Yes, plan on coming up in June." She was emphatic about this, so even though I felt a heart tug to be there, I agreed.

But that conversation had happened the day before. Today's would be much different.

"Stacey Lynn?" said the male voice on the phone.

Before I could respond, he said, "It's your daddy."

My mind at this point was several seconds behind. I recognized the deep voice of my Uncle Larry. His next three words sent me into a tailspin.

"He is gone." His voice choked out the words, but they were clear enough for me to know what he had said. Still, I said what you would expect me to say.

"What?"

"He passed this morning, honey. I'm so sorry."

At this point a sound deep from within my soul escaped before I could contain it. I heard it. I felt it. I saw it. But I could not stop it. I jumped up and started pacing back and forth around my bedroom.

I set my phone down and continued to pace around the room. This became my before-and-after moment. *Before* the phone call I was making plans for shopping, pool sitting, and movie watching with my girls. *After* the call I was swimming in an ocean of grief in desperate need of something to grab on to.

The room was spinning. The combination of shock and grief laid me low, and I parked my shaking body on the floor against the wall next to my bed. I didn't move for at least an hour. I'd had the wind knocked out of me once as a girl and woke up on the floor of my neighbor's garage, struggling to breathe. Now, some forty years later, I was on the floor, knocked clean out, struggling to breathe, and trying to figure out what had happened. Being in the wilderness hurt deeply, and I had been caught off guard in every way.

*Growth doesn't happen at Disney World; it
happens in the hard places of our lives.*

After I tried five times to reach my husband in as many minutes, he returned my call. He knew something must be wrong. I told him what happened, and a friend of his brought him immediately to our house. When my husband arrived home, he asked me what I knew and I told him. At the time I didn't know much, only that my dad was gone. We found out later he collapsed at home from what we think was a pulmonary embolism. My dad died suddenly and without pain just after kissing my mom and sending her out the door to her eye doctor appointment. He told her to get gas because the price was going up the next day. Which of course it did, because Daddy always knew things like that.

I told my husband, "I don't know what to do next." He, in the calmest voice possible, said, "We just have to do the next thing."

He brought me a Diet Coke and a turkey sandwich.

We told the girls.

We cried.

We prayed as a family.

I spoke with my brother and my mom in what can only be described as the hardest conversations I have ever had in my life—and the next thing I knew it was dinnertime. Life was moving in fast-forward and slow motion simultaneously, and I wasn't sure if I was coming or going.

Later that night I found myself standing in the Loft. I don't really remember driving there. It was after their closing time, and I must have looked a bit lost. The kind salesgirl asked me what I needed, and I said, "A dress." She did not question me or complain about my sneaking in at two minutes past nine. I left with a lovely black dress and a sweet pink cardigan. As I hung them in my car, I started to cry. I had just picked out the dress for my dad's funeral. That morning I had thought I would be at the beach this week. Life had changed so suddenly.

As minister and writer Matthew Henry once said, "Those whom God has mercy in store for he first brings into a wilderness."[2] I can tell you straight up that my plunge into the wilderness of grief did not feel like fresh mercy on day one or even on day seventeen. But God led me there, and it wasn't to watch me bleed for nothing. He had a purpose in my pain. He always does.

> You shall remember the whole way that the LORD your God has led you these forty years in the wilderness, that he might *humble you, testing you to know what was in your heart,* whether you would keep his commandments or not. And he humbled you and let you hunger and fed you with manna, which you did not know, nor did your fathers know, that he might make you know that man does not live by bread alone, but man lives by *every word that comes from the mouth of the* LORD (Deuteronomy 8:2-3).

This wilderness stripped me. I was humbled and dependent, crying out to God for my next breath. I had no choice but to beg him for it. During those early days of grief, nothing else held any hope whatsoever. What came out of my heart in those early days looked a whole lot like bitterness, and my gracious God absorbed every drop. Sweetly, he began to speak to me there, and he used the most precious people to do so.

Bouleversement

My friend Kathleen told me later that what I was experiencing was a *bouleversement*. This French word means "a total upheaval, an upset, an absolute reorientation of the way you saw the world before." She said, "That's what you have ahead of you. I and so many others in the family of Christ will be praying you through the agony, the blur, the chaos as you try to figure out a world without your father in it."

Yes. Yes. Yes. That is where I was. In the blur.

And somehow in the blur, we packed all six of us into our van and drove for two days to Indiana to be with my mom, brother, sister-in-law, and other family members and friends. We mourned deeply and I kept doing the next thing I had to do, one thing at a time. Another dear friend, Lisa-Jo, told me, "Stacey, the only way through is through. No matter what, you have to go through it. And you will. And God will hold you together because that is what he does. He holds everything together, and everything includes you" (Colossians 1:17).

But I didn't want to go through. I didn't want to look through thousands of pictures and remember. I didn't want to stand at the funeral home for five hours straight. I didn't even want to think. What I really wanted to do was escape. I had the strangest desire to go to Disney World. I wanted for a while to feel magical and good and happy. Even if it wasn't real, I wanted to suspend reality for a few minutes.

Of course, growth doesn't happen at Disney World; it happens in the hard places of our lives. The messy places don't run through *It's a Small World* with happy little working songs. *Through* is through the chaos of grief. What my friends Lisa-Jo and Kathleen both knew was that the only way to make it through grief was to let Jesus hold you together. He would. I could trust him to do that because of his promise. They knew this not because they read books or watched sad movies. They learned it in the pit of their own suffering—in saying goodbye, in crying real tears, and inside their own *bouleverse-ment* moments.

It was the truth from Colossians 1:17 that rose to the top and took me with it. I'll tell you I have done everything with these words from holding on for dear life, to wrestling them, and finally standing firm. Truth is true no matter how you feel. And it made all the difference in the world during the most turbulent ride of my life.

> I will give her her vineyards from thence, and the val-
> ley of Achor for a door of hope: and she shall sing there
> (Hosea 2:15 KJV).

My family asked me to sing at Daddy's funeral, and I couldn't. No way. It is virtually impossible to sing when you are weeping. Do you know your throat actually closes up and you can't sing? It's true. Besides, the song was nowhere to be found.

In the early days of grief, my worship pastor, Jon, said, "Don't lose your song, Stacey." How did he know I was so close to letting bitterness swallow up my song? I had no idea how to respond to Jon. I'm a worshipper. I lead worship. I love to sing. The trouble was, when I tried to sing after my daddy died, the lyrics got stuck in my throat. When that phone call came, I started swallowing song lyrics, and they were balm to my heart. Yet even today, singing about heaven stops me mid-note.

But God had promised, "She will sing there." His people came out of Egypt singing songs of deliverance, and the God who enabled those songs promised that this bitter place, this valley of Achor, would also be filled with a song. He had promised, and I was holding on to that promise with both hands. Quite frankly, though, the song in my heart was really more bitter than sweet.

From One Bitter Woman to Another

Naomi knew the valley of bitterness. We often miss bitter Naomi starring in her own story because we only see her daughter-in-law Ruth. And Ruth is the girl we want to grab coffee with—she's the show-up kind of friend we all pray to have. Ruth is worthy of our study for sure, but I've grown to love Naomi in a fresh new way because she understands my bitterness. Don't give me quaint Bible stories when my heart is shattered into a million tiny pieces. Give me a gritty girl who's been there. Give me a woman who knows what my friend Kathleen knew, who knows the *bouleversement* and had survived.

Naomi's Valley of Achor

Stories like Naomi's make us want to look away. Hers wasn't pretty in the beginning, and it kept getting worse. In order to understand the depth of Naomi's pain, we need to do our best to see things from her perspective. Getting some of the backstory will help.

Naomi's valley of Achor began when a famine struck her hometown of Bethlehem where she lived with her husband, Elimelech, and their two sons. The famine must have been pretty severe because hunger moved this family to a bountiful land called Moab. Easy decision, right? "We have no food here in Bethlehem, so let's flee our circumstances and go to a place where there is food." The problem for them, however, was that God had forbidden his people—and that included Elimelech and Naomi—to go to Moab. This foreign land was enemy territory: God had drawn a boundary around Moab and said explicitly of this land and this people, "Don't go there." Elimelech's family went anyway.

Now, I promise you I am not sharing this backstory with you to cast Naomi and her family in a bad light. I get the fleeing! I completely understand the desire to escape difficult circumstances. I understand the powerful temptation of bountiful land when you are weary and fresh out of amazing. I just call that land Target or Starbucks, and I run there not because my family has nothing to eat. I run there because I am overwhelmed with life. Now, God hasn't called Target or Starbucks enemy territory, but they could become that if I use them to escape a difficult set of circumstances. God wants me to lean into him during days when my soul feels famished, not run to retail therapy or fancy coffee drinks that help me pretend

I don't have any problems. Whipped topping is sweet but it doesn't really do much for the state of my heart.

Naomi and her family, now living in Moab, solved one problem: They were no longer hungry. But soon after they arrived in Moab, a series of devastating events began that would cause Naomi to later say this:

> Do not call me Naomi; call me Mara, for the Almighty has dealt very bitterly with me. I went away full, and the LORD has brought me back empty. Why call me Naomi, when the LORD has testified against me and the Almighty has brought calamity upon me? (Ruth 1:20-21).

So what happened? First of all, Elimelech died, leaving Naomi widowed in a foreign land. Sometime later, her sons, Mahlon and Chilion, married:

> These took Moabite wives; the name of the one was Orpah and the name of the other Ruth. They lived there about ten years, and both Mahlon and Chilion died, so that the woman was left without her two sons and her husband (Ruth 1:4-5).

These ten years of living in Moab left Naomi bitter, not bountiful. The Voice translation of Ruth 1:21 says, "I left this place full, *in spite of the famine,* but the Eternal has brought me back empty *from a plentiful land.*" Did you catch that? She was full in a place experiencing a famine. And she finds herself empty in a plentiful land. No wonder she refused to be called Naomi, which means "pleasant." She wanted to be called Mara, which means "bitter." She was saying in essence, "Every time you say my name, be reminded, I'm bitter." They probably didn't need a reminder. Naomi didn't hide her bitterness.

For just a minute let's sit here with Naomi in her valley of Achor. This wilderness has broken her. Could she be anymore fresh out of amazing than she was right now when she returned to Bethlehem? Perhaps the words of Psalm 88:6-7 (THE VOICE) capture what she surely was feeling:

> [I'm] forsaken *by Him* and cut off from His hand,
>   abandoned among the dead who rest in their
>   graves.
> And You have sent me to be forgotten with them,
>   in the lowest pits *of the earth,*
>   in the darkest canyons *of the ocean.*
> You crush me with Your anger.
>   You crash against me like the *relentless, angry* sea.

The psalmist and Naomi had feelings I understand, especially the part about grief being a *relentless, angry sea.* For some reason, grief came to me in images of water too. Initially, I felt like I was in an ocean of grief. Sounds were muffled, life was happening all around me, and I was immersed and floating in it all. Then, grief came more like waves crashing on the shore. Steadily crashing over me again and again, grief sometimes rolled over me when I least expected it, like when I was paying for my groceries or driving down the street.

But God did not leave me alone. He gave me his own water-filled promise: "He provides me rest in rich, green fields beside streams of refreshing water. *He soothes my fears*" (Psalm 23:2 THE VOICE). Could the crashing waves ever be refreshing water? I was more than a little skeptical, but pastor, teacher, and writer John Piper made this observation:

> Here is the question the book [of Ruth] answers: Is God's
> bitter providence the last word?...The issue for real peo-
> ple in real life is, Can I trust and love the God who has
> dealt me this painful hand in life?[3]

This was the question Naomi had to answer. God had allowed a bitter chapter in her story, and he allowed one in mine too. One thing God was going to teach her in the wilderness of her pain, though, was that even in the darkest of days, he was present with her and acting on her behalf. He was working. He was providing. And, yes, she could trust him.

Naomi's Door of Hope

I discovered Hosea 2:14-15—the verses that opened this chapter—when I was in the middle of my wilderness of grief. A precious blog reader sent them to me, and they provided me with a tiny spark of hope. Funny, I had turned in the *Hope for the Weary Mom* manuscript only a few weeks before I lost my dad, and now I needed my own hope stirred up. Grief can swallow you whole and take your memory with it. I slowly worked through the verses and then wrote this in my journal: "God is in the business of turning valleys of trouble into gateways that lead to acres of hope." I wrote these words by faith, because at the time I just didn't see the gateway leading to anything but more grief. But praise be to God! With gentleness and grace, he swings wide open the door of hope when we need it most. Naomi's door of hope swung wide open too. If she'd had eyes to see, she would have noticed the tiny sparks of hope gleaming on the other side.

The Spark of Not-Alone

God used Naomi's circumstances to draw her home. There was nothing left for her in Moab. I'm not sure she longed for God, or if she was returning home to die, still clinging to her bitterness and grief. Either way, she set out on her journey back to Bethlehem accompanied by her two daughters-in-law, Orpah and Ruth, yet in every way Naomi was still alone. Do you know that you can be in a room full of people and still feel the sting of loneliness?

They traveled for a while when Naomi turned to them to send them away. Three times she said, "Go back!" She pleaded with them to return to Moab and their families. As she urged them to go, they wept and wept again. Finally, in a decisive moment, Orpah turned back; Ruth, however, clung to Naomi, declaring her fierce commitment to her:

> Do not urge me to leave you or to return from following you. For where you go I will go, and where you lodge I will lodge. Your people shall be my people, and your God my God. Where you die I will die, and there will I be buried. May the LORD do so to me and more also if anything but death parts me from you (Ruth 1:16-17).

You've probably heard this tender speech voiced at wedding ceremonies by love-struck brides and grooms, but it was first proclaimed by one widow to another in the face of bitter emptiness.

The presence of a friend can encourage us to not turn back in grief, but to look forward with hope.

Naomi's response to Ruth's pledge of loyalty was less than warm and welcoming. When she saw that Ruth was bravely determined to go with her, Naomi consented with nothing more than, basically, a "Suit yourself." John Piper says this of Ruth: "Naomi painted the future very dark, and Ruth took her hand and walked into it with her. Ruth's commitment to her destitute mother-in-law is simply astonishing."[4] Later the two women entered Bethlehem together, and Naomi disregarded Ruth's presence when she told the townspeople she had returned empty.

But Naomi wasn't empty. She may have had the sense to return but in her grief almost missed the sweet provision God had given her in Ruth—the spark of hope that said, "You are not alone." The power of *I will go with you* speaks volumes even without Ruth's bold speech. So much so, we still remember her words today, all these years later.

When my dad passed away, I was deeply touched by how many people came to pay their respects and to love on our family. Many of my friends drove for hours to be with us. I had little to offer them: I was numb and wet with tears, trying to be strong for my mom as well as my girls. These precious people came anyway, and their presence thoroughly blessed me. A couple of my friends, Lisa and Robin, went above and beyond merely coming to pay their respects: they lingered. I first saw them on Saturday afternoon during the calling hours. They were weeping as they made their way through the long line to my family. We sat down with other sweet sisters for a few minutes at the end of the evening and talked about the events of the week. That support was all that I expected from them or anyone else. They were part of a dear group of women who showed up for me, and I was truly blessed by their love.

The next day was the funeral. When I got to the church with my family, Lisa and Robin were there, seated to my right. They sat together, still weeping. At one point, they rescued me with tissues when I was bottoming out with the ugly cry. After the service, they said they were blessed to be a witness to the testimonies about my dad. I said goodbye and slid into the driver's seat of my mom's vehicle to start the slow, steady journey to the cemetery. The graveside service would be short, reserved for family and a few of my dad's closest friends. I sat at the front with my mom, my brother and his wife, and my husband and said my last goodbye. When I stood up to hug my aunt, I noticed that Lisa and Robin were standing off to the side, a few gracious steps back, grieving with us. *They came to the cemetery*. I went to them and said, "I can't believe you came here too."

They hadn't come for my dad, though they knew him. They came to strongly support me in my darkest hour. I was undone by the gift of their quiet presence. They and so many others were like

Ruth to me. The presence of a friend can encourage us to not turn back in grief, but to look forward with hope.

The Spark of Bread

> What she [Naomi] does not see with the eyes of her heart is that in all her bitter experiences, God is plotting for her glory. This is true of all God's children. In the darkest of our times, God is plotting for our glory. If we would believe this and remember it, we would not be as blind as Naomi was when God began to reveal his grace.[5]

God loved Naomi. While she was letting bitterness eat away at her insides, God was busy plotting for her glory. He was about to unfold his grace, and it looked a lot like bread in the beginning. (I'm convinced bread is a love language all its own. Don't even try to argue with me on that.)

> Naomi returned, and Ruth the Moabite her daughter-in-law with her, who returned from the country of Moab. And they came to Bethlehem at the beginning of barley harvest (Ruth 1:22).

If you read through the book of Ruth too quickly, you might miss this verse at the end of chapter 1. I know you really want to get to the part about Boaz and Ruth. We all love the romantic parts of the story. But this one sentence is power-packed with hope, and we simply can't skip over it. God is in the details of our lives, and in those details he shines bright.

In the Hebrew language *Bethlehem* means "house of bread."[6] For years, however, this House of Bread suffered a famine, and there was no bread at all. But when Naomi walked into town, the barley harvest was just beginning. The House of Bread would have bread again. Two women of famine were about to reap a harvest they had not sown. A bitter Naomi had headed home, but God went before her. His grace was at work ahead of Naomi and Ruth as the seeds went into the ground, the rains came to cause them to grow, and the sun tenderly encouraged them to blossom. God positioned workers to faithfully tend to the fields to protect them until just the right time for harvesting—and for Ruth and Naomi to arrive. God plotted Ruth and Naomi's glory with perfect timing.

This moment in Ruth's and Naomi's stories reminds me of Psalm 27:13: "I would have despaired unless I had believed that I would see the goodness of the LORD in the land of the living" (NASB). The goodness of the Lord had visited Bethlehem, making it once again the land of the living, and at the point Naomi was most despairing, God revealed it to her. God is so good to do the same for us: He plots our glory, sends workers ahead of us, and reveals to us his goodness.

But back to Ruth and Naomi. Can you sense hope rising at this point of their story?

The Spark of a Future and a Hope

Recently I watched an interview of Erin French, owner of the Lost Kitchen, a restaurant in a small town in Maine. Erin had experienced great culinary success in the big city a few years ago and was riding high on fame...until one day she lost everything, including her marriage. She moved home with her parents and was not sure what to do. Out of desperation she began to cook again, going back to her roots of farm-to-table cooking. Soon, she had a thriving business in a small trailer financed by her parents. Today, she has a beautiful, rustic space in an old sawmill that overflows with guests nightly. She said of her journey, "When it felt like everything was falling apart, it was really just falling into place."[7]

Naomi had felt "like everything was falling apart," but now everything was about to fall into place. God always has a plan, and it is always infused with hope. It didn't matter one bit that Naomi was fresh out of amazing. God was not limited by the state of her heart. His glory and grace juxtaposed against her dark life of bitterness made this chapter of her life only more astounding. It is God who moves both mountains and us to show us the beauty of his plan. God was plotting Naomi's glory and was ready to bless her with his bountiful provision. She had nothing to bring to the table, and he was about to fill it with more than just bread.

As it turned out, Naomi and Ruth's spark of a future and hope rested with a relative named Boaz. He was a man of wealth in every way that mattered. He possessed not only land but a heart for God. At every turn—and as he positioned himself to care for Naomi and her daughter-in-law Ruth—he demonstrated God's own passion for the weak, broken, and unworthy. He also knew the law that provided for a widow to be cared for by her late husband's nearest kinsman. If that man were willing, he could rescue and redeem a widow from her poverty by making her his wife. Boaz became that kinsman-redeemer for Ruth and, by extension, for Naomi.

God carved Naomi's path back to Bethlehem with a foreign daughter-in-law whom she had tried to send away. He ordained her course to intersect with Boaz, who responded to his God-given responsibility as a kinsman-redeemer. Boaz protected and provided for Ruth and Naomi. This story takes my breath away because God does precisely the same thing for us.

In this story of Ruth and Naomi, I hear hope singing like this:

> What amazing things the LORD has done...
> Yes, the LORD has done amazing things for us!
>   What joy!
> Restore our fortunes, LORD,
>   as streams renew the desert.
> Those who plant in tears
>   will harvest with shouts of joy.
> They weep as they go to plant their seed,
>   but they sing as they return with the harvest
>   (Psalm 126:2-6 NLT).

The Lord restored their fortunes and renewed the desert places in their lives. They harvested with shouts of joy when Ruth gave birth to a son. As they placed this tiny baby in Naomi's arms, the women gathered around her with words of joy:

> Blessed be the LORD, who has not left you this day without a redeemer, and may his name be renowned in Israel! He shall be to you a restorer of life and a nourisher of your old age, for your daughter-in-law who loves you, who is more to you than seven sons, has given birth to him...A son has been born to Naomi." They named him Obed. He was the father of Jesse, the father of David (Ruth 4:14-15,17).

And in that glorious moment, as the song of hope was being sung all around her, I think Naomi surely must have been wiping tears of gratitude from her cheeks. Her grieving had given way to hope.

Seasons

> For everything *that happens in life*—there is a season, a
> right time for everything under heaven:
>   A time to be born, a time to die;
> a time to plant, a time to collect the harvest;
>   A time to kill, a time to heal;
> a time to tear down, a time to build up;
>   A time to cry, a time to laugh;
> a time to mourn, a time to dance.
>   Ecclesiastes 3:1-4 THE VOICE

We stayed with my mom until we absolutely couldn't anymore. It was simply time to return to our home in Florida because of work and school. She was in good hands, and even though I knew it, leaving my mom was like jumping off a cliff. Both my husband and I drove back: I was in the van and, because my mom wanted him to have it, my husband drove my dad's pick-up truck. My girls made great copilots, and in my harder moments, they sang me songs, and we laughed through tears. This was the best medicine.

The first morning back at home I grabbed my oversized cup of coffee and sank down deep into the red chair where I meet with Jesus every morning. Of course he was there waiting for me just as he always is. I had much to say to him, and I'm grateful that he graciously absorbed it all. I told him in no uncertain terms that I was done, I had nothing left to give to anyone, I didn't have any encouraging words to put on my blog or care about making a new book outline. I wanted to sit in that big chair forever and pull the blanket over my head. I wanted to quit life. I wanted to be bitter like Naomi. In many ways I was. I told my heavenly Father, "Lord, I'm fresh out of amazing in every way."

And what I heard in that moment in the depths of my heart was "Jesus loves me." This was a new season for me. One I had never found myself in before. I was about to experience what Charles Spurgeon said, "The seasons change and you change, but your Lord abides evermore the same, and the streams of His love are as deep, as broad, and as full as ever."[8] My ocean of grief was not as deep as the love my heavenly Father has for me. And his love is the one thing that will never change.

Then, as if Jesus himself were sitting next to me in the red chair, I heard him say, "I know you feel fresh out of amazing, sweet girl. But do not fear. I do not waste anything you experience in your life. You are exactly where I want you. I am never out of amazing—and it's time for you to see me big in your life."

Tears streamed down my face, and I picked up my Bible. At the Spirit's leading, I turned to a tiny book in the Old Testament called Habakkuk. It was time for me to begin the process of healing. It was slow in coming, but in the light of dawn on that April morning, healing quietly began. My own sweet and bitter experience of God's providence was unfolding in a song.

Part 2

The Invitation

Invitations can be quite a big deal, especially when you get married. I'm sure my husband and I viewed at least five hundred different designs for our wedding invitations. In the end, we chose a fairly simple style: a white embossed card featuring black lettering. It took us several days to craft the perfect wording—we wanted to give a nod to the traditional yet have our own personal touch. Of course we put the mandatory piece of tissue paper on top of the card because we didn't want our invitation to rub against the envelope and get blurry. After all, it was important our guests knew when and where to go for our ceremony. Our reception was simple, so we did not require an additional RSVP card. (Maybe someday I'll tell you all about how we had Kentucky Fried Chicken for our guests at our reception and everyone loved it. But that is a story for another time.)

We spent more time on that wedding invitation than on any other invitation we had ever or will ever send out. I know people like to make a fuss over first birthdays and graduations. Since we really just gave our babies a personal cake and said, "Dig in" we never needed one. Graduation may well be a different story because our girls have big Pinterest-type expectations. Thankfully, graduation is a couple more years away for our family.

Invitations can be simple too. My friend Kristin has started something beautiful and simple right in her front yard. She parked a basic wooden picnic table a few feet from her door and painted it the most beautiful shade of turquoise. Everyone in her neighborhood knows when Kristin is sitting at the Turquoise Table, they have an open invitation to join her. Today, thousands of Turquoise Tables are popping up all across America (Virginia, Texas) and around the world (Africa), and hearts are connecting. It is a movement of hospitality that says, "You are welcome here." I love it.

Jesus gives the ultimate invitation when he says, "Come and follow me." It isn't elaborate, but it is layered with life-changing meaning for the person who accepts it. You simply can't say yes to Jesus and stay the same. He has a way of radically rearranging the hearts of his followers. When Jesus's first followers said yes to him, they saw him do marvelous things. Hearts were healed, multitudes were fed, and the dead came back from the grave. I think he wants to do the same marvelous things for us today.

Dear, sweet, fresh-out-of-amazing girl, this is your invitation to see God big. He wants to move us toward him. You have a decision to make: You can stay where you are, or you can move forward with faith. I believe that because you have waded this far into the book, you are ready for God to work in your life so you can see him big. I know I am.

So let's take a deep breath and see where God wants us to follow him in the days ahead. Much of part 2 is super practical, and I hope you will find it a useful and encouraging tool. My prayer is, when you close the pages of this book, your heart will be more in love with the One who is always amazing. He is the One who changes us.

Chapter 7

Wrestling

O LORD, how long shall I cry for help, and you will not hear?
HABAKKUK 1:2

We don't really get any sweet introductions to the prophet Habakkuk. Instead we get one sentence packed with passion. We also see, at the beginning of the book that bears his name, that Habakkuk was feeling the full weight of some burden and crying out to the Lord. It seems pretty obvious that he didn't feel like God was listening to his petitions about said burden. In fact, the entire first chapter of his story reads like the pages of the book you hold in your hands: Habakkuk was fresh out of amazing. He wanted God to do something to change his circumstances. When he finally did hear from God, Habakkuk complained because what he heard wasn't really what he had in mind.

He asked how long.

He asked why.

He complained.

Sound familiar? I hope you said yes because this first chapter of Habakkuk, save a few key historical details, could have been taken from my personal journal. I totally get Habakkuk the burdened prophet. Maybe that is why the Lord gently led me here in the first place.

Habakkuk was crying out to God and wrestling with him. Appropriately, his name means "to wrestle." (My name, if you are interested, means "resurrection." This is slightly more encouraging than "to wrestle.") In 1971 I don't think my parents gave much thought to the meaning of my name, but it is good to know if someone writes about me in the future, my name doesn't mean "to yell loudly when no one pays attention to her." (Not that I ever do that, of course.)

Living up to his name, Habakkuk the wrestler was wrestling with God. Habakkuk was trying to understand the living God he served. You see, God was about to send one of Israel's worst and most evil enemies upon them to pretty much devour them. As a prophet, Habakkuk had to tell the people about this pending judgment. I guess we can understand why he was so worked up and wrestling the Almighty. I don't think Habakkuk was out of line. More importantly, I don't get the impression that God was broken up about the wrestling prophet asking tough questions. And Habakkuk didn't sugarcoat them one bit:

> God, you're from eternity, aren't you?
> Holy God, we aren't going to die, are we?
> God, you chose *Babylonians* for your judgment work?
> Rock-Solid God, you gave *them* the job of discipline?
> But you can't be serious!
> *You* can't condone evil!
> So why don't you do something about this?
> Why are you silent *now?*
> This outrage! Evil men swallow up the righteous
> and you stand around and *watch!* (Habakkuk 1:12-13
> MSG).

You are God aren't you? You can't be serious? Why don't you do something about this? Why are you silent? God can take the questions

Habakkuk was asking. Aren't you glad about that? I know I am because lately I have been asking more than a few questions myself.

My Own Wrestling

Early one spring morning I found myself making the best of a chair beside my daughter Caroline's hospital bed. She was sleeping; I was not. Instead, I was wrestling with God in my pit of despair. It felt like I was drowning while standing on dry ground. I had no eloquent words. No verses rose up from the hundreds I could have recited the day before. The only thing I could remember was the story of the centurion who went to Jesus and begged healing for his servant. The centurion told Jesus that it wasn't necessary for him to come to the house: "Only say the word, and my servant will be healed" (Matthew 8:8). So, like a woman long ago and, I'm sure, countless since then, I grabbed hold of his holy hem and would not let go.

Over and over I prayed it: *Just say the word, Jesus.*

I had been shaken to the core—and for good reason. The day before I had stood in front of about thirty or so women and talked about the *marathon of motherhood* and how God goes before us and makes provision for our every need. I believe that with all my heart. I truly do. But when the doctor calls at midnight that same night and tells you to go to the ER because your daughter's hemoglobin is dangerously low, you do it. You wrap her in her pink blanket, grab her favorite bear, and you go. When they lead you to a pediatric intensive care unit and your baby girl is sick for who knows why, your clever words aren't much comfort. You wrestle with why, you wrestle with how long, and you wrestle with the silence.

I can tell you, the silence in a tiny hospital room at four o'clock in the morning is deafening. All I had in that moment was the One who had promised to hold me together. And I was holding on to him with everything I had. It wasn't much. It was small. Gratefully, God works not because of what I bring to the moment, but because of who he is. He was enough that night, and he will always be enough.

A doctor's diagnosis comes slowly. Or at least it comes much more slowly than moms and dads would like. As the puzzle pieces began to fit together and our eight-year-old endured just about every test you can imagine, we found some answers. Those answers came with treatment I was nervous to say yes to. They also came with a large dose of mommy guilt I had to battle, because how could I not have known? What kind of mother does not know this is happening right under her nose? I wrestled with that too. Maybe I still am.

But the doctor spoke the words I longed to hear. In my heart, though, it was really Jesus who confirmed it: "She is very sick, but she is going to be okay."

And something deep within this weary mom broke wide open after I had held my breath for hours that seemed like days. And Jesus held strong. Because what is truer in the moment than his promise to never leave us and his call to take courage in him? Nothing.

God bore witness to my wrestling no one saw. He didn't hide from me; he held me.

Eight days in a hospital dismantles what you know and feel about life. It changes your priorities. We were humbled and grateful to be released to go home with a diagnosis she could live with. It could have turned out so differently. And if it had, God would still be good, and God would still be enough.

God is not surprised by midnight phone calls to rush our babies to the ER, the passing of his saints, or the world's rages or quakes.

Our God is the one thing we need in such times and always. He can handle his people's questions whether they're asked by prophets of old or moms worried sick over their babies. Author Angie Smith once said on her Instagram, "There is something beautiful about the wrestling nobody sees." Is it possible God looked down and saw my ache, my desperation, and said, "Beautiful"? He bore witness to my wrestling no one saw. He didn't hide from me; he held me.

We All Wrestle

We will get back to talking about the wrestling prophet Habakkuk, I promise. We have so much to learn from him. But I can't help but guess what you might be thinking, "What about me? I wrestle too." Rest assured: You are not alone. All fresh-out-of-amazing girls wrestle. Ultimately God wants to use our wrestling for our good. The point of a wrestling season is for us to surrender to our heavenly Father, not to win. But first we need to understand the different ways we wrestle. By discovering the wrestler living inside of us, we will be able to see our starting point. This will help us get to where we want to go faster. Nobody in her right mind wants to wrestle forever. Ain't nobody got time for that.

What Type of Wrestler Am I?

I was thinking that maybe we could keep this simple and have two categories of wrestlers. In one corner we would have the Internal Team of wrestlers and in the other corner we would meet the External wrestlers. But the more I thought about it, the more clearly I could see at least four different types of wrestlers emerging. As you read through these four categories, I think you will quickly assess where you fit. (I'll tell you where I fit after I introduce you to these four folks.) Because we need to keep things a little light-hearted around here, I thought it might be more fun to make up wrestling names for each type. I mean, how could I resist?

The Internal Team

The Research-a-Nator. "I am a thinker who is often lost in her own thoughts. Some people might call me an intellectual. I am always doing research, looking for more information. I mean, can you ever gather too much? When I wrestle with God, it is because I don't know enough. I want to 'know before I go' because that's the smart thing to do."

Sheza the Emotimizer. "I experience the entire range of human emotions. I could name them one by one. I am content to take in and process wave after wave of my swirling emotions. At times I think I could sit for hours and pour out my heart in poetry. A perfect day for me would be sitting in a trendy coffee shop during a rain shower listening to sad and soothing songs. When I wrestle with God, it is because I need to feel safe and secure before I will trust him with my heart."

The External Team

The Crusader. "Do you need someone to get up and do something? I'm your girl. I am concerned deeply about issues, and I can't help but try to save the day. I won't be found sitting around idle when something is bothering me. Social injustices? I'm against all of them in Jesus's name. Of course I wrestle with God, but I find it better just to move on and be a force for good."

Insta-Girl. "People are awesome. They really are. I have so many friends online I can't keep up with all of them! I'm a connecter and relator who shares everything everyday with all the people in my world. If I'm wrestling with God about something that really matters, I will talk to my friends about it first. I once wrote a Facebook post about a problem I was having, and people were so great. They prayed for me. I felt better because they knew I was having a tough time. It helped me to know I was not so alone."

Internal Team	External Team
The Research-a-Nator I'm a thinker Intellectual Know before I go	**The Crusader** I care deeply about the issues Doer Be the good
Sheza the Emotimizer I feel all the feelings Emotional Need to feel safe	**Insta-Girl** I love people Connector Tell me what you think

It is entirely possible that you might find a little bit of your wrestling heart parked in different categories at various times in your life. I definitely see that in the life of David. He wrestled with God. David was a creative who penned beautiful heartfelt words to the Lord. But he was also a leader who often crusaded and rushed to fix rather than merely feel. So don't see these four types as neat little boxes. We human beings are far too complex to be only one forever. Right?

Which description would you say fits your current struggle? As promised, I'll answer first. It might not come as a surprise to you that I'm mostly Insta-Girl with a dash of Sheza thrown in: I feel all the things, I have some trust issues with God, and I wonder in the depths of my heart if he really does care about me right here, right now. When I'm wavering and afraid to let go of what I am holding too tightly, I seek the opinions of friends: I invite group therapy with *Please, somebody fix me. Pray for me. Help me.* I love to let others cast their votes on which way I should go or what I should do. I want someone to just stand up and say, "Hey, girl! This is going to be okay. Really! Trust God!" Wrestling can feel dreadfully lonely. When others affirm my struggle, I feel validated for some reason. Does that make sense?

Maybe you do a completely different type of wrestling. But for each of us, our ultimate surrender is always an attitude of the heart. Knowing where our hearts tend to drift will, in the long run, help us move toward a place where we are ready to hear from the Lord and obey.

The Very Real Struggle of Prayer

I don't want us to move on too quickly and miss a key fact in this passage. Habakkuk's entire struggle takes place in a conversation of prayer. He is praying to God, and he is struggling at an all-time breaking point. Meanwhile, the people in the land are wicked, and justice has essentially vanished. The prophet is done. Finished. Why is God not doing something? After all, he is God. Habakkuk said, "O LORD, how long shall I cry for help, and you will not hear?" (1:2). Can you hear the stress in his words? The Hebrew word for *cry* is the word *shava*. It means "to cry out, to shout."[1]

Habakkuk was not offering a quiet bedtime prayer. He was shouting to God with the same intensity used by fellow believers—by Job when his whole world crumbled; by Jonah, from the belly of a whale; and by David, when he penned Psalm 31, the very psalm Jesus echoed from the cross.

If I hadn't been in a hospital at four in the morning, I would have shouted my prayer too. Friends, the *shava* of our hearts draws a response from our Father in heaven just as it did for the heroes of our faith. But like Habakkuk, we tend to get frustrated when our answers are not immediate or a course we would choose ourselves. We want God to answer us on our time schedule. Never mind the fact that often we come to God after we have exhausted every other resource in our lives.

I really want to sound spiritual right now and say, "I'm a first line of defense prayer warrior for sure. Yeah, you bet I am!" But in reality, I'm more of a "try everything else first and then pray" type of girl. I know better. I really do. God has told us that he meets us in the *shava* of surrender. Which, for me, feels a lot like weakness. Maybe that's why I struggle so much. But God firmly addressed this matter through Paul's words in the New Testament:

> Finally [God] said to me, "My grace is enough to cover and sustain you. My power is made perfect in weakness." *So ask me about my thorn,* inquire about my weaknesses, and I will gladly go on and on—*I would rather stake my claim in these* and have the power of the Anointed One at home within me (2 Corinthians 12:9 THE VOICE).

Don't miss these key points:

- It is in our weakness that God's power is made perfect.
- It is in our surrender that God's own Spirit within us cries out, "Abba!" to the Father (see Romans 8:15-16).
- God comes to us.
- God ministers to us deep within our hearts.

Wouldn't it be easier to start at this point of surrender? So what if today, we came to the end of ourselves first thing in the morning instead of fighting our way to 10:00 a.m. or 3:00 p.m. or 8:45 p.m.?

What if, by prayer, we staked our claim into the ground of our weakest spot, that place where we break every day, and truly let his power be at home there?

After all, we are *his daughters*.

His *grace* covers us always.

His *power is made perfect* in our weakness and imperfections.

In this place where I break, God breaks through.

The *shava* of our hearts draws a response from our
Father in heaven just as it did for the heroes of our faith.

Why, How, and Who

I think wrestling is a *why* place. When we look back at what
Habakkuk said, we can definitely hear him say between the lines,
"Why are you letting this happen, God?" We like to know *why*,
don't we? Habakkuk was no different from you and me. But you
know what I've realized? God doesn't usually answer our *why* ques-
tions no matter how many times we ask. So is it a sin to ask why?
Elisabeth Elliot shared this in one of my favorite books, *Keep a
Quiet Heart*:

> It is always best to go first for our answers to Jesus Him-
> self. He cried out on the cross, "My God, my God, why
> have You forsaken me?" It was a human cry, a cry of des-
> peration springing from His heart's agony at the pros-
> pect of being put into the hands of wicked men and
> actually becoming sin for you and me. We can never suf-
> fer anything like that, yet we do at times feel forsaken
> and cry, *Why, Lord?*[2]

Does it bring a bit of relief to know that Jesus himself didn't get
a firm answer? I'm so glad we have a God who knew how important to our faith—to our relationship with him—it was to put on
flesh. Jesus—God with flesh—hung on the cross and cried out. God
heard his *shava*. You and I can ask why. Jesus himself did, but in the
end, he still trusted and yielded to the will of his father. This has to
be our resolve as well.

In addition to being a *why* place, wrestling is also a *how* place. When I was sitting in the hospital with my daughter, I wanted to know how God was going to fix her body. I also wanted to know, should the diagnosis be more than I could bear, how I was going to get through it. I certainly wanted to know how I was going to be strong for my baby girl when she was scared and hurting. *How, Lord? How are you going to move in this situation?* My *how* questions opened the door of my heart just enough to let fear creep in and make those moments even more intense. Remember my saying that I felt like I was drowning on dry land? Fear takes great delight in our feeling like that.

As I waited on the Lord to tell me how the situation would be resolved, I also wondered what I was supposed to do. There isn't much to do when you are sitting beside a hospital bed. Maybe that was the point all along. Watchman Nee explained this profoundly:

> When you cease doing, then God will begin. Have you ever tried to save a drowning man? The trouble is that his fear prevents him trusting himself to you. When that is so, there are just two ways of going about it. Either you must knock him unconscious and then drag him to the shore, or else you must leave him to struggle and shout until his strength gives way before you go to his rescue. If you try to save him while he has any strength left, he will clutch at you in his terror and drag you under, and both he and you will be lost. God is waiting for your store of strength to be utterly exhausted before he can deliver you. Once you have ceased to struggle, he will do everything. God is waiting for you to despair.[3]

Friend, is it possible that God has actually been waiting for you and me to be fresh out of amazing? Has he been patiently observing all our efforts to fix situations and save ourselves while knowing all along that, at some point, we would exhaust all our strength? Is it possible that once we have ceased wrestling with *why* and *how*, he will do everything?

In this place where I break, God breaks through.

I think Habakkuk wrestled with *why* and *how* until he came to the understanding of *who* he was really wrestling with. I think he exhausted his own strength and realized God had only just begun to display his. How do I know this? In the beginning of the next chapter, Habakkuk surrendered. He said, "I will take my stand at my watchpost and station myself on the tower, and look out to see what he will say to me, and what I will answer concerning my complaint" (2:1). I don't think Habakkuk said it calmly. I like to think he threw up his hands and said, "Fine. I'll go. I'll wait. I'll listen." I think Habakkuk still had questions. But his wrestling had finally come up against the reality of *who* God is:

- Everlasting (1:12)
- Holy (1:12)
- The Rock (1:12)
- "You who are of purer eyes" (1:13)
- Creator (1:14)

Yes, Habakkuk surrendered. Will we?

I recently read this from Kelly Minter: "This place of surrender is the most freeing of places to be and the hardest to get to. Some of us have been working, toiling, and struggling. We've done all we can do, and now it's time to cease striving and lie down at the feet of Jesus."[4]

Girls, I get it. I get the working and toiling. I also get the eye rolling you secretly do when you are fresh out of amazing and someone pulls out the Bible bullet "Be still, and know that I am God" (Psalm 46:10). But I want to tell you something I wholeheartedly believe: You've done all you can do. You can keep wrestling if you want to. God will wait until you're finished. But admit it. Don't freedom and stillness sound so much better than more wrestling?

It is high time we ceased all the doing and let God work.

Exhale, girl.

I'm right here with you.

Chapter 8

Watch and Wait

*I will take my stand at my watchpost and station myself
on the tower, and look out to see what he will say to
me, and what I will answer concerning my complaint.*

HABAKKUK 2:1

*D*efining moments may be beautiful to watch, but they can be terrifying to live through. We love the fact that, after wrestling with God throughout the entire first chapter, Habakkuk surrendered to him. But now we are sitting on the edge of our seats because we want to see, "Does God come through? What's going to happen next? And what in the world is a watchpost anyway?" We want to know the rest of Habakkuk's story because we are trying to decide for ourselves what we should be doing. We might also be wondering what our defining moment is going to look like. And maybe, just maybe, if Habakkuk makes it through to the other side in one piece, we can too.

If this were a movie, I would put it on pause and probably run to the kitchen to refill my diet soda and grab some extra M&M's or popcorn. One can never be too snack-ready during a defining moment. And this is a huge moment for Habakkuk. I sense something big is going to happen. Don't you? Do you have your appropriate snacks nearby? This single verse teaches that Habakkuk's defining moment is all about perspective, positioning, and patience. Let's go to the watchpost with Habakkuk and see what else we can learn.

Perspective

Habakkuk was in great need of perspective. He was willing to do just about anything to see God clearly. Desperate to have greater vision for God's plan, he said he would go to the watchpost. You might be wondering the same thing I was when I first studied this passage: What is a watchpost? Because, really, when was the last time you said, "Hey, honey! I'm heading out to the watchpost. Be back in an hour—or three days!"

A watchpost is a small sheltered tower usually standing in the middle of a vineyard. During harvest time, farmers would go to the watchpost to protect their ready-for-harvest crops. Because the watchpost stood tall in the vineyard, farmers could see for miles around. They could be sure the workers were actually working and no one was trying to steal their grapes. Usually, during the harvest season, the farmer and his entire family moved out to the watchpost and lived there. Every farmer worth his salt would have a watchpost—which leads me to think that Habakkuk made a living as a farmer. You see, being a prophet wasn't exactly profitable. So Habakkuk had a watchpost because he was a farmer by trade.

According to Dr. Ed Bez, the watchpost (or tower) symbolized something else as well:

> Watchtowers are also used figuratively throughout scripture. The watchtower was a symbol of [God's] strength, providence, and protection. As well, the watchtower and its watchman are symbols of prophetically keen individuals anointed by the LORD to be guardians of the times and seasons.[1]

I don't think Habakkuk went to the watchpost because he was worried about the grape harvest. I think he went to the watchpost to get alone with God and gain some perspective. It was a physical place, but it had great spiritual significance for him. For Habakkuk, going to the watchpost was an act of the will. He would not be idle; he would go to the watchpost, and he would see what God was going to say. Habakkuk was saying with his actions, "God, I want to see you, and I want to have your eyes for my people. If I'm going to deliver your truth to them, I need to see what you see." Habakkuk's watchpost was a place where he could get away from the pull of earthly things, a place where he was raised up, fixed his eyes on heaven, and saw clearly.

Where is your watchpost, friend? Mine looks less like a tower and more like an oversized red chair I sit in most mornings to meet with God. I always have a warm cup of coffee when I sit in my watchpost because in order to be quiet, I have to get up very early in the morning. It is not uncommon for my youngest to climb into my watchpost with me when she gets out of bed. Sometimes she snuggles up next to me and falls back asleep. While she sleeps beside me, I open God's Word and read. I pray. I love meeting with him in my watchpost. On occasion, when my day needs to start super early, I have to rearrange my watchpost time to later in the day or else miss it altogether. Can I tell you something? My heart aches when the latter happens. My watchpost has become a sacred space where I see God. It is the place where he consistently unveils my eyes and sets my gaze upon his will for my life.

I have learned, however, not to romanticize my watchpost. I often do gritty work there. Habakkuk probably wasn't singing "Kumbaya" and painting a vineyard landscape while he was camped out in his watchpost.

After my dad died, I lingered in my watchpost each morning to look at my grief through the pages of God's Word. I can assure you in those early days of grief, I was wholeheartedly fixing my attention on the Lord. I was longing to see him and gain his perspective on my heartache and loss.

All this talk of watchposts reminds me of an article I read about Britain's mysterious Stonehenge. Located just north of Salisbury, England, this group of stones stands as one of the wonders of the ancient world. For years, archaeologists have wondered what these stones represent, why they are there, and whether or not the stones once formed a complete circle. They may have found the answer due to a dryer-than-usual summer in 2013. When a grounds-keeper noticed some parched spots on the monument's southwest side, archaeologists investigated. An aerial view of those dry spots supports the longstanding speculation that at one time the stones made a circle.

> Susan Greaney, the senior proprieties historian for Eng-lish Heritage, explained to the BBC that the grass at Stonehenge is watered during dry spells in the summer, "but our hosepipe doesn't reach to the other side of the stone circle. If we'd had a longer hosepipe, we might not have been able to see them," she said.[2]

It took a dry season and a short hosepipe to shed some light on the Stonehenge mystery. I'm pretty sure the groundskeeper would have called these inconveniences, and he might have even grumbled about the situation. But, without them, even the experts would not have had eyes to see the truth.

Sweet friend, God uses dry seasons and short hosepipes in our lives too. How better to describe being fresh out of amazing? A dry season might just be the very thing it takes to get us to climb into our watchpost and beg God to let us truly see what we haven't been able to see before. God understands the way we are made, and I think he uses our real-life circumstances to create a longing to see him.

Positioning

The perspective gained in the watchpost is about seeing God; the positioning is about hearing from God. I love the fact that Habakkuk was absolutely convinced God was going to speak to him. Notice what he said: "I will take my stand at my watchpost and station myself on the tower and look out to see *what he will say to me*" (2:1). He did not say, "*If* he will speak." He knew it is God's nature to speak to his people. Habakkuk needed to put himself in a position to listen.

A while back I led a Bible study of twelve women who gathered every Monday for three years to grow in their relationship with God and to hear him speak to their hearts. They were a little apprehensive when the study called for us to read *The Pursuit of God,* one of my favorite A.W. Tozer books. (I might be putting it mildly when I say I am a raging Tozer fan.) I assured the women that once they waded through the first few pages, they would be hooked. By the time we got to chapter 6, "The Speaking Voice," we were all raging Tozer fans, mostly because he wrote things like this:

> God is forever seeking to speak Himself out to His creation. The whole Bible supports this idea. God is speaking. Not God spoke, but *God is speaking*. He is, by His nature, continuously articulate. He fills the world with His speaking voice.[3]

The God who fills the world with his voice spoke to Habakkuk, and he speaks to us too. Isn't that astounding? The women in my Bible study were particularly moved by this discussion. *God speaks to us.* Who are we that he would speak to us? We are normal everyday girls who rush through the drive-thru at Starbucks. We might be moms with sticky floors. We go grocery shopping, for crying out loud. Yet *God* speaks to *us*. Why would he do that? Because he created our hearts to need to hear him.

Tozer went on to say, "The Word of God affects the hearts of all men as light to the soul."[4] His Word *is* light to our soul. It illuminates the parts we wish were hidden from the world and especially from him. It chases away the darkness. His Word directs us. Quite frankly, it challenges us. But it also gives us great hope. Where would we be without it, friend? We would be stifled by the silence and wondering which way to turn.

Habakkuk did not have the luxury of cracking open his Bible and reading God's written Word like we do. But God spoke to his heart that was positioned on his watchpost to hear his Lord speak. Habakkuk was saying, "I'm here, God. I'm ready to listen."

God speaks to *us*. Why would he do that? Because he created our hearts to need to hear him.

My busy preschooler is our own personal Tigger, constantly in motion. Sometimes I need to give her important instructions like "Don't jump on the couch. You might crack your head open." To ensure I have her undivided attention, I grab her precious face in my hands and make eye contact with her. I have to say, "Baby, are you listening to the words Mommy is saying? Can you repeat back to me what I said?" We have our own version of the watchpost moment when she is able to tell me precisely what I said. Then I release her with a kiss on the head, and she goes back to bouncing. This is what I imagine God was doing spiritually with Habakkuk. The prophet had positioned himself to listen to God. He stopped what he was doing, went to his watchpost, and gave God his undivided attention. Then God took his holy hands, placed them on Habakkuk, and spoke. God desires to do that for us as well.

And of course Tozer has something good to say about this:

> If you would follow on to know the Lord, come at once
> to the open Bible expecting it to speak to you. Do not
> come with the notion that it is a thing which you may
> push around at your convenience. It is more than a thing,
> it is a voice, a word, the very Word of the living God.[5]

Oh girls, what our fresh-out-of-amazing hearts need more than anything else is to hear the voice of God. Let's not push his Word aside one minute longer. Let's go to the watchpost and listen expectantly. Let's marvel at what he says. We will not climb down out of our watchpost the same girls we were when we entered. We will be changed. Glory, what an invitation!

Patience

Watchposts are for perspective and positioning, for seeing and hearing, and for growing our patience. If only we could make the seeing and the hearing happen when we are at our most desperate! But the truth remains: God speaks on his own schedule. I think we wish with all our hearts God would stand up and say, "Wow! Stacey has gone to the watchpost! I'm not going to waste any of her time. I'm going to just say what needs to be said so she can move on with her life." That might be more efficient for us, but our eternal and holy God has a bigger picture in mind.

God certainly speaks, but as we are waiting to hear him, he is producing something beautiful in us as well.

> There's more to come: We continue to shout our praise
> even when we're hemmed in with troubles, because we
> know how troubles can develop passionate patience in
> us, and how that patience in turn forges the tempered
> steel of virtue, keeping us alert for whatever God will
> do next. In alert expectancy such as this, we're never
> left feeling shortchanged. Quite the contrary—we can't

round up enough containers to hold everything God
generously pours into our lives through the Holy Spirit
(Romans 5:3-5 MSG).

As we wait for God to speak to us, he grows in us the steel vir-
tue of endurance. Like it or not, we don't develop endurance easily.
The passage above says endurance is *forged*. A forge is where metal
is heated to the point where it is malleable and sometimes even liq-
uid. A craftsman takes the metal, softened by the heat, and ham-
mers away until he forms the object of his desire.

Developing patient endurance in us is no different. It takes a little heat and a lot of hammering until we are malleable. Remember I
said the watchpost can be a gritty workplace? I can't think of a grit-
tier work than the forging of a patient heart. But don't lose hope.
God does not make us wait a minute longer than we need to.

⌒

Watch closely and know that the waiting
days can be a season to savor.

⌒

Thirteen years ago when I first moved to Central Florida, I was
in a season of waiting. I waited for friendships to develop. I waited
to be familiar with my new town. I waited to feel at home in my
large church. Everything about my life was a matter of waiting on
the Lord to do something. During that time, I dug deep into my
relationship with God, and that's when he gave me a promise that I
think needs to go on the walls of all of our watchposts:

Behold, I am doing a new thing;
now it springs forth, do you not perceive it?

> I will make a way in the wilderness
> and rivers in the desert (Isaiah 43:19).

You see, as God was forging in me a patient heart and refining my character, he was at the same time wooing me with words of promise and comfort. He was preparing me for the new things he was about to do in my life. Guess what? At just the right time, friendships blossomed, my house became a home, and my church became a family.

Today, as you stand in your watchpost, God is doing the very same thing for you. He is growing your endurance as you wait. He is wooing you with tender promises. He is preparing those new things for you and you for those new things. It is happening. I assure you. Watch closely and know that the waiting days can be a season to savor. He is coming just over the horizon. You can trust in God's perfect timing.

Pushing the Pause Button

Sometimes our desperation drives us to the watchpost because our hearts are hungry to hear and see God. Of course we need to be sensitive to the Spirit. Habakkuk certainly was when he declared he would go to the watchpost to watch, listen, and wait. But wouldn't it be fruitful to also plan for times of watching and waiting? Keep in mind the farmer's watchpost time marked a specific season. When the grapes on the vine were ready, the farmer moved to the watchpost. (The grape harvest season extended from June to September.)

Our watchpost season could be a purposeful time of bountiful harvest for our souls as well. In doing so, we could push the "pause" button of our lives and seek after God's heart. I heard Nancy DeMoss say on her podcast, "You don't drift into intimacy with Christ; you drift away from intimacy with Christ. If we're not being intentional in cultivating that love relationship with Him, we are going to drift away."[6] Instead of drifting away, we could go to our watchpost to:

- Take stock of our lives
- Look to see where the enemy might be stealing our joy
- Adjust our attitude
- Cultivate our love relationship with Christ
- Refresh our hearts after a time of intense ministry
- Restore our vision for God's plan for our life
- Take a Sabbath rest for our souls

When I was writing this chapter I happened to be taking a girls' weekend with my college friends. We have gathered every year for the past twenty-two years. These women are not only dear friends, but are passionate followers of Jesus, active in all kinds of ministry. I shared these ideas about the watchpost with them, and immediately they began talking about how it reminded them of our need for rest. Then my friend Unchong shared a story from Mark Buchanan's book *The Rest of God*. He described rest by using a beautiful scene from J.R.R. Tolkien's *The Lord of the Rings*:

> In book 1 of *The Lord of the Rings Trilogy*, [Tolkien] describes a time of rest and healing in the house of Elrond in Rivendell. The hobbits, along with Strider, their guide, have made a dangerous, almost fatal journey to this place. They will soon have to make an even more dangerous, almost certainly fatal journey away from this place. But in the meantime, this: "For a while the hobbits continued to talk and think of the past journey and of the perils that lay ahead; but such was the virtue of the land of Rivendell that soon all fear and anxiety was lifted from their minds. The future, good or ill, was not forgotten, but ceased to have power over the present. Health and hope grew strong in them, and they were content with each day as it came, taking pleasure in every meal, and in every word and song."[7]

All fear and anxiety was lifted from their minds...Health and hope grew strong in them. Doesn't that sound like heaven on earth? Sign me up immediately! I'm beginning to think the watchpost could be like the land of Rivendell for us.

We all need rest and healing, and those can be difficult to find. Unchong went on to share with me her struggle:

> By nature, I'm a doer. I love efficiency, productivity, achieving things. When I was in the process of reading [*The Rest of God*], I was in the throes of busyness, which was really eating away at my soul-wellness. I was awakened to the reality that I don't experience rest, and the outcome was that I really didn't care anymore. I had to cut some things out of our lives, but I also really needed a tangible rest day per week and an ongoing posture of rest for my spirit.
>
> After chewing on the idea of rest, I began to set aside Sundays after church as a time to just do things that are restful and or refreshing. It takes faith to do that, weirdly, because it involves actively saying no to just doing one load of laundry. It also required planning, so that Sunday could be the day I don't cook. We reserved our once-a-week eat-out day to be Sunday, or I made dinner on Saturday to feed us Sunday. That's the everyday life stuff.
>
> In a counterintuitive way, I had to practice more discipline to experience this soul-restfulness. It's *really* hard for me to go to bed at a decent hour, but I had to force myself (I have many relapses) to go to bed early enough so that I can get up early enough to work out and meet with Jesus, sipping my coffee. As a busy mom, I've found no other way to consistently cultivate my walk with Jesus apart from getting my time in the Word in before my family's day gets going. But it has a huge payoff. The act of discipline by faith enables me to experience restfulness in God.

As Unchong shared this with me, my heart totally understood. I confess, I struggle big time in this same area. I'm guessing you do as well. Women often feel like they need to get permission to do anything that has a hint of leisure to it. But God wired us to need downtime as part of the rhythm of our lives. Watching and waiting takes a commitment and sometimes an act of the will. Unchong discovered it took great discipline to push the pause button, but the payoff was worth it. Still, the invitation is ours to receive...or not.

And the invitation sounds a lot like these words that Jesus spoke. I mentioned them once before in chapter two during our discussion of Martha. Honestly, they are so good I think they warrant repeating here:

> Are you tired? Worn out? Burned out on religion? Come to me. Get away with me and you'll recover your life. I'll show you how to take a real rest. Walk with me and work with me—watch how I do it. Learn the unforced rhythms of grace. I won't lay anything heavy or ill-fitting on you. Keep company with me and you'll learn to live freely and lightly (Matthew 11:28-30 MSG).

Watchposts give us a glorious chance to push the pause button, keep company with Jesus, experience real rest, and lean into the unforced rhythms of grace. Time in our watchpost brings perspective when we need to see as God sees and watch how he works.

Watchposts also provide the position from which we will best hear God when he speaks. His promise is not to give us anything too burdensome because he bears the weight of it. Yes, the work can also be gritty, but it is worth it. I have a gut feeling the reason Habakkuk went to the watchpost in the first place is because he made a habit of going every year. It was a refuge, a tower of strength, and, in the simplest of terms, a place to be with God.

I don't know about you, but this place to be with God and rest is what my heart is absolutely longing for. I want to pretend I am a child again, playing hide-and-go-seek in my neighbor's backyard on a sultry summer night. I want to slip off my tennis shoes and, dodging fireflies as I go, run as fast as I can to the watchpost. I want to yell, "Home free!" when I get there and sink down onto the porch glider. There is no better place to be.

Habakkuk leads us by example: He was in his watchpost and, as expected, God spoke. What God said includes a couple instructions I find completely fascinating. I can't wait to dive into this with you in the next few pages. That being said, if you find yourself loving and lingering in the watchpost, I completely understand. Join me in the next chapter only when you are good and ready.

Chapter 9

Write It Down

*And the LORD answered me: "Write the vision; make
it plain on tablets, so he may run who reads it."*

Though I may never come down solidly on how to pronounce
Habakkuk's name, I feel he and I are somehow bonded for
life. We've witnessed him wrestle his heart inside out in the posture
of prayer. Together we have scaled the watchpost to watch and wait
for God to speak. We've fixed our eyes on the horizon, and, with
Habakkuk, we've strained our ears to listen for the Lord's voice. This
farmer-prophet has grabbed my heart. Maybe you feel the same way.
If so, you will understand me when I say the verse above made me
want to shout "Hallelujah!" and give Habakkuk a fist bump or two.

First, the statement "the LORD answered me" is no small thing.
God spoke to Habakkuk. Did you doubt that he would? I think
I pretty much expected God to speak because, you know, this is
the Bible after all. But when I'm waiting on the Lord, I certainly
don't always have the same confidence in my own heart that the
Lord will speak to me. This verse is such an encouragement to me
because Habakkuk heard God speak specifically to him about the
matter at hand. Not only that, but God gave him a to-do list. You

should probably know this brings me great joy. As a type A, people-pleasing girl, I just love to know exactly what is expected of me. In college, my favorite day was always syllabus day: "Here are sixty-five days of readings and assignments. Do them and pass my class." It didn't matter that I had to read ten books and write seventeen papers. Knowing what I had to do left me with a feeling of control. And don't get me started on reading with a highlighter in hand. I could go on and on about that awesome invention. I will, however, contain my excitement because we have more important things to discuss.

> When God speaks, we don't need to
> dress it up or make it fancy. His Word, his
> vision, his instructions are enough.

What did God tell Habakkuk to do? He told the prophet to pick up the chisel and record the vision on a tablet. God also told him how to do it. The phrase "keep it simple" is the Hebrew word *ba'ar*, which means "to explain, declare, and dig out the sense (or meaning)."[1] This same Hebrew word appears two other times in Scripture. *Ba'ar* was first used when Moses *spoke* the law to the Israelites on the banks of the Jordan near Moab. The word was also used when God told Moses to *write* the law for them on stone tablets. By his own confession, Moses was a man of few words. He spoke simply, and God wanted him to write simply. (I've always heard it is more authentic to write like you speak, so this instruction makes perfect sense to me.)

Now consider that God had to tell farmer-turned-prophet Habakkuk to keep his message simple. He didn't have a hashtag, images purchased from iStock, or even colored pens to make his message extra special. He didn't have a Journaling Bible or a You-Tube video. He had a simple message written on tablets of stone and God said, "Hey, Habakkuk, just write what you saw. Nothing less. Nothing more." When God speaks we don't need to dress it up or make it fancy. His Word, his vision, his instructions are enough:

> The Word is always plain and clear. It is not written in code. It is not the hiding of God, but the Revelation of God. The Book of God is spiritual, but it is not complicated. Without question, it is a sealed Book to those who believe not. But for those who have eyes to see, ears to hear, and hearts to believe, the Revelation of God is clear.[2]

The clear vision God gave to Habakkuk is not revealed to us here, so we are left guessing what it might be. God did tell Habakkuk that the vision was for an "appointed time" in the future, and it is a fairly safe bet that Habakkuk was referring to the coming of Christ. The gospel is lingering here in this tiny book of the Old Testament for those *who have eyes to see and ears to hear it*. Habakkuk himself reminded us that "the righteous shall live by his faith" (2:4). The vision he recorded was going to happen after Habakkuk left this earth. He would spend the rest of his days living by faith that God would not delay in fulfilling what he had revealed.

I wonder if, after he chiseled out the message, Habakkuk uttered those words as an affirmation for his own heart. I like to think that may be the case because writing down a message God has for me sure has an affirming effect on me. In fact, I happen to believe this is a valuable application for all of us to consider.

Writing for Our Souls

Now, I know what you may be thinking: "But I'm not a writer. I failed writing in college. I avoid writing grocery lists. I'm going to skip this next section." Before you move on, though, let me just put this out there for you to consider:

- Habakkuk was a farmer.
- Peter was a fisherman.
- David was a shepherd.
- Matthew was a tax collector.
- James was a carpenter.
- I am a mom.

You don't have to identify as a writer to write down faith-affirming words inspired by God. You simply have to be willing. And whether anyone sees your words or you tuck them away in a journal like I did for years, your words matter because your soul matters. Author Julie Cameron puts it this way:

> We should write because it is human nature to write. Writing claims our world. It makes it directly and specifically our own. We should write because writing brings clarity and passion to the act of living. Writing is sensual, experiential, grounding. We should write because writing is good for the soul. We should write because writing yields a body of work, a felt path through the world we live in.[3]

Writing is indeed clarifying soul work. And isn't that what we need most when we are fresh out of amazing? When I am feeling it deep down in my dry, dry bones, I need to make sense of the world and my place in it. I want to bring back the passion I have for God and for living for him. I want my soul to sing again. Writing slows down the very fast-paced world we live in and reorients our innermost being to the Lord. If we want to claim our world and revive our passion, as Cameron says, we have to slow it down by writing our way through it.

Whether anyone sees your words or you tuck them away
in a journal, your words matter because your soul matters.

Looking back, I see that words have always been important to
me. I communicate, I talk, and I always have. In third grade, let's
just say citizenship was not my best grade. Did you have citizenship grades? If not, you should know this was a grade based on your
behavior. I said words all the time, which should give you some indi-
cation of what my grade might have been.

During my middle school years, words began to pour out in a
new way. I put words on wide-ruled notebook paper, folded them
into fun shapes, and handed them to my best friend, Carrie, in the
hallway. They were words about life, music, cheerleading, and boys.

When I was in college, my words were timid. A small-town girl
on a Big Ten Campus doesn't have much confidence in what she
writes on the page. During my freshman year, my English profes-
sor confirmed that lack of confidence with searing words that made
me want to hide. Still, I wrote. I spelled out my deepest thoughts in
fabric-covered journals. During these years my writing took more
the form of one continual prayer conversation with the Lord.

When I moved to a far-off place in my early thirties, I put my
words in letters and sent them to friends back home. They sent back
to me words of encouragement that gave me strength. I put their
notes and letters on my refrigerator door and cried every time I read
them. Words have always been like friends to me, and when flesh-
and-blood friends could not be there, their words brought great
comfort.

As I've mentioned, a few years back, I sat around a table to study
God's Word with other women. We shared life and grace for three

years. At the close of our journey we wrote words to one another and read them aloud. Tear-stained pages have never been so beautiful. Over and over again the women in the study said to me, "You are a writer. You should be writing." Writing was becoming a calling on my life I could not ignore.

My husband echoed that idea when he said, "You should blog. You need to be writing." But I wondered what I would say—and who in the world would care what I said anyway! One day I took a leap of faith, typed my first word, and a few minutes later hit "publish." Somewhere along the way, I learned I don't write because I have all the answers. I write because I do not.

Writing for Our Growth

Our Creator God wants to minister to our souls, grow us in the hard places, and teach us something as well. Writing down words, as it turns out, is an excellent way for us to learn. Hear what Stanislas Dehaene, a psychologist at the Collège de France in Paris, found:

> When we write, a unique neural circuit is automatically activated. There is a core recognition of the gesture in the written word, a sort of recognition by mental simulation in your brain. And it seems that this circuit is contributing in unique ways we didn't realize. Learning is made easier.[4]

Learning made easier? I'm all for that, aren't you? The psychology minor in me is so intrigued by this article. I hope you are too. If not, bear with me a few more minutes. I promise this is leading somewhere.

The article goes on to say that even the messy figures your kids make on their kindergarten papers are valuable. (This gives me great hope because sometimes I think my own handwriting looks a bit like my five-year-old's—or even worse.) Research has shown that handwriting makes what we learn stick around longer:

Two psychologists, Pam A. Mueller of Princeton and Daniel M. Oppenheimer of the University of California, Los Angeles, have reported that in both laboratory settings and real-world classrooms, students learn better when they take notes by hand than when they type on a keyboard. Contrary to earlier studies attributing the difference to the distracting effects of computers, the new research suggests that writing by hand allows the student to process a lecture's contents and reframe it—a process of reflection and manipulation that can lead to better understanding and memory encoding.[5]

It may seem simplistic, but I believe Habakkuk's model works for us here. If the Lord speaks to me, I want to remember what he said. I want to recall how I was feeling when he spoke. I want to know the date and where I was sitting when he said it. (Was I sitting at Starbucks or was I writing in my journal after I read from the book of Psalms?) And if God in his wisdom desires to teach me something while he is speaking to me, I want to learn it as easily as I can. Being fresh out of amazing can be sweet and fertile ground for God to do a mighty work in us and through us. This has certainly been true for me.

On the day *Hope for the Weary Mom* was born, I was literally sitting in a laundry pile when God prompted me to begin writing. Looking back I can see he wanted me to write my way out of the fog I was in. He wanted to teach me something about how to have hope in the daily grind of life. He wanted that truth to anchor my soul to the promises he had for me in his Word. In his grace, God also allowed those words to encourage other women along the way. If I had not been listening to God and writing down what he was teaching me, I'm not sure my time with him would have benefitted me as much. The very act of writing helped me to remember the moment. And if I hadn't, I'm confident the thousands of women who have read the pages of *Hope for the Weary Mom* would not have had the opportunity to walk with me through my harder days. Writing it down also produced a hope-filled work as God met me in my own mess. The writing process turned out to be a beautiful work of redemption for me and for so many like me. I am humbled beyond words that God blessed me with a Habakkuk moment, a time when I heard him speak both hope and direction into my life.

Preaching the gospel to my heart every day is a moment I savor, a moment that reaps great dividends in my life.

Is it possible, my friend, that this is your Habakkuk moment? Could it be that God has brought you to your own spiritual watchpost to whisper to your heart as well? Let me challenge you to pick up a pen or open your laptop and start writing right where you are. Make your words a prayer to God. Don't write with any intention of doing anything with it. Just listen on the page and let God meet you there. And if you happen to be in a laundry pile, be encouraged. He does good work there too.

To Savor

It is no secret that I have a deep love of a good cup of coffee, and I'm a firm believer in having at least one cup per child every day. The fact that my new coffeepot brews before I wake up each morning is my own personal version of Disney World. Coffee is my happy place. But over the past year or so, I've been learning the art of drinking a cup of tea as well. I used the word *art* for a reason, and the reason is, art refuses to be rushed. There is something beautiful about the slow steep of my favorite *Sweet and Spicy* blend, the swirling of the cream, and the dollop of whipped topping I add to make mine more like a dessert. I usually grab my favorite mug, climb into my oversized chair, and take time with my tea. I'm not drinking it to survive my day—which is why I drink my coffee. I'm drinking tea to slow down and savor the moment. According to the Merriam-Webster Dictionary, *to savor* means "to enjoy something for a long time." I grab coffee on the go, but tea is for sitting and savoring. This is probably why it has taken me my whole life to actually become a tea drinker. I've finally found the sweet spot of the savoring life.

We can savor words God gives us in much the same way that we sip a cup of hot tea: slowly, purposefully, and with enjoyment. I think the best place to tuck away words worth savoring is a daily journal. As we write the words God speaks, we turn our gaze inward to the work our hearts need the most. David Mathis of the *Desiring God* blog says this:

> Journaling is an opportunity to preach the gospel freshly to yourself, beginning where you are, without simply feeding yourself the canned lines of truth you'll default to without pausing to think and to write it out.[6]

Do you know what I need most when my heart is fresh out of amazing? I need to preach the gospel to myself. I need to hear *loved, chosen, rescued,* and *forgiven.* I need to remember that Jesus—by his death and resurrection—has already broken every chain that holds me back from living my life to the fullest in him. I need to declare to myself that Jesus alone can supply the power I need to accomplish the mission he has given me for my life. Amen?

Preaching the gospel to my heart every day is a moment I savor, a moment that enriches my life. Preaching God's truth to myself personalizes the message and stirs up hope in my heart. Psalm 34:8 encourages us to "taste and see that the LORD is good! Blessed is the man who takes refuge in him!" It is in savoring his words that we are able to live out this verse and receive his comfort.

We too easily forget the fact that God wants to work *in* us before he works *through* us. Journaling allows us to mark these moments when he speaks to us and teaches us. Journaling helps us remember the tender works of God in our hearts. Without a record, those moments will fade and be forgotten. Journaling ensures that we will always have a memorial of those times we met with and heard from God. What a beautiful record for our souls!

Something else happens when we pay close attention to our inward life. Inevitably, we are moved to take steps of faith we might never have taken otherwise. I have also found journaling to be a beautiful birthplace of ministry to others. Do you know where I first put to words my dream of writing a book? It was on the pages of a worn-thin journal in which I used to hold one-on-one conversations with the Lord. Discussing the book with him privately laid the foundation I needed to move forward. David Mathis agrees: "Writing doesn't merely capture what's already inside us, but in the very act of writing, we enable our heads and hearts to take the next step, then two, then ten."[7]

What is the next step you need to take? Writing about it might be the best place to begin. I can promise you God is a secret-keeper and a dream-giver. He won't post your innermost thoughts on Facebook, but he just might give you the faith to be so bold and do it yourself.

To Say

Sometimes we need to savor the words God gives. We need to sit with his message meant specifically for our hearts and let it have its full effect. But at other times, like in the case of Habakkuk, we need to be bold and say the message simply and out loud for all to hear. It doesn't have to be complicated for you to write it down with the intention of sharing it with others. Could you send an encouraging note or read part of your journal to a hurting friend? How about posting your favorite Bible verse on your favorite social media platform?

We open our hearts, and from the beginning God begins to mark it with his holy pen. He writes Christ on it, telling those who read our lives that we are his.

My pastor, David Uth, gave an impassioned plea recently for us to see social media as the primary language of our day and to boldly proclaim the message of Jesus Christ every time we share something. He said, "What would happen in our circle of influence and around the world if we used social media for the glory of God?" The truth is, if we are active on Facebook, Twitter, or Instagram, we are all published authors with searchable content. Wouldn't it be something if people pulled up our personal feed and saw the Word of God written all over it? What if we shared our stories and pointed to his grace every day? I think other believers would be encouraged, and nonbelievers might take notice that our God is worth writing about.

The Best Place to Write

Maybe you think this journaling idea is fine for word-loving girls, but you still do not consider yourself a writer. Perhaps even keeping a private journal has no appeal to you. I have had times in my life when my journal sits unused and gathers dust. I get the "no appeal." I really do. But guess what? *Friend, we are the actual living letters other people are reading.* The apostle Paul said it in 2 Corinthians 3:2-3 (The Voice):

> You are our letter, every word burned onto our hearts to be read by everyone. You are the living letter of the Anointed One, *the Liberating King,* nurtured by us and inscribed, not with ink, but with the Spirit of the living

God—*a letter too passionate* to be chiseled onto stone tablets, but *emblazoned* upon the human heart.

We open our heart and from the beginning God begins to mark it with his holy pen. He writes Christ on it, telling those who read our lives that we are his. God doesn't write on stone tablets anymore. He writes on human hearts that live and breathe and have their being in him.

And as we go about our day, our hearts bump into the hearts of others, and we write a message on their hearts as well. When we write God's grace words, we build up, love, and encourage the people we encounter. It gives me pause to think of the hearts I have written on today. What mark did I leave? Have I left a God word there for others to read? Will my marks on their hearts point others to Him? The most powerful place to write God's truth is on the tablet of someone's heart. We have to treat this responsibility with great care.

Sharing the gospel is simply writing *Jesus* on the heart of everyone we encounter. When we do that, people will not say, "She is amazing!" They will say, "Wow! Her God is good."

Remember the gospel truth we savored and preached to our own hearts earlier? His first marks on our hearts read:

- Mine
- Daughter
- Grace lavished

- Loved
- Forgiven
- Lovely

Do my marks on others echo that?

As a writer, I often think about the effect of words. But I hope after considering the ideas in this chapter, you understand that you are a writer too. It is tempting when we are fresh out of amazing to only write messages of discouragement and discontent on the hearts of others. But sharing the gospel is simply writing *Jesus* on the heart of everyone we encounter. When we do that, people will not say, "She is amazing!" They will say, "Wow! Her God is good." Your words, if chosen carefully, can land in the soft places of people's hearts and point them to Jesus. I'm overwhelmed by this opportunity he so freely gives. It is truly sacred space.

A Writer's Prayer

I shared this prayer on my blog last year, and it truly reflects the desire of my heart when I write. I think it is appropriate and even crucial that, before we pick up our pens and write, we commit each and every word to Christ. Would you join me in speaking this over your own words?

Lord,

First make me a listener. Give me ears to hear what you are speaking. Shut out the noise all around me and let it be your voice that rises above every other sound.

I ask for eyes to see the world brand-new every day. Let the miraculous lovely rise up out of the crazy busy and may it be like a snapshot of life frozen before me. May I see it. May I see You, daily.

Help me, Jesus, to never stop learning what you are teaching me. Let me always sit in the classroom of your grace. I ask you to write every lesson on my heart.

And when I do write, give me the gift of hesitation with consideration. Remind me, Lord, to take a holy pause before I publish anything—be it a blog post, a letter, a tweet, a status, or anything else.

Inspire my heart.

Move my hands.

Be glorified—always—in my words.

Amen.

Chapter 10

Worship: Even If...I Still Will

*I have heard the reports about You, and I am in
awe when I consider all You have done.*

HABAKKUK 3:1 THE VOICE

I have a confession to make. Remember in chapter 7 when I told
you Habakkuk's name means "to wrestle"? Well, that is absolutely true. But I didn't tell you the entire meaning of his name. I
wanted to save the best part for last.

Think of it like this: I just offered you a delicious chocolate
brownie, which you devoured in ten seconds flat. After you chased
it down with a cup of cold milk, declaring it to be the best brownie
you have ever eaten, I said, "Can you believe I made it with zucchini?" You would gasp and say, "No way." But then you would ask
for another. You could have a second helping because this brownie
is basically a chocolate vegetable. I think you would be glad I didn't
tell you in the first place about the whole zucchini thing. Now, you
love me even more for waiting to surprise you with the second guilt-
free brownie you just ate.

This confession is just like that except without the brownie.

So I felt like it would be better to save the second part of the
meaning of Habakkuk's name for this chapter. I could have told

you before, but you probably would have glossed over it without much thought. I don't think it would have meant much to you a few chapters ago. But now that we've really gotten to know Habakkuk, the full meaning of his name is going to be a sweet treat for your heart. This is—in the words of the late Paul Harvey—"the rest of the story."

Part 1 of Habakkuk's story features him as the wrestling prophet. We love that part of the story because we, too, wrestle with God and his plan for our lives. With each verse we say, "What? You too, Habakkuk?" Who knew we had so much in common with a prophet who lived so long ago?

Part 2 of Habakkuk's story highlights the second meaning of his name, which is "to embrace." The wrestler becomes the embracer right before our eyes, but it doesn't happen instantaneously. This story is a journey. Because there is a beautiful progression here, I would love to unpack that with you for the next few pages. Ultimately, as you will see, Habakkuk embraces a heart of worship. But what does Habakkuk embrace to prepare his heart for the climax?

Embracing Faith

The heart of Habakkuk's message is his declaration of faith in God no matter the circumstances. The prophet said, "The righteous shall live by his faith" (2:4). Warren Wiersbe said this:

> Habakkuk teaches us to face our doubts and questions honestly, take them humbly to the Lord, wait for His Word to teach us, and then worship Him no matter how we feel or what we see. God doesn't always change the circumstances, but He can change us to meet the circumstances. That's what it means to live by faith.[1]

This small verse in the tiny book of Habakkuk—"the righteous shall live by his faith"—is referenced three times in the New Testament.

- The righteousness of God is revealed from faith for faith, as it is written, "The righteous shall live by faith" (Romans 1:17).

- It is evident that no one is justified before God by the law, for "The righteous shall live by faith" (Galatians 3:11).

- My righteous one shall live by faith, and if he shrinks back, my soul has no pleasure in him (Hebrews 10:38).

Habakkuk was a living example of a faith that questions and complains, but who did not shrink back. He pressed forward in faith. Oh, girls, we can too. Do you have more questions than answers? Are you fresh out of amazing today without a clue where God is leading? Faith makes it possible to look forward with hope. It is the foundation for anything we will ever encounter. Let's embrace faith in our God this moment, no matter what may come.

Embracing Silence

In the midst of declaring his faith, Habakkuk was once again made aware of the evil in the world around him. Isn't that usually the case? When we take a stand for Jesus, the whole world looks like it is doing its level best to defy God. Habakkuk seemed to ramble on and on about "soul empty" men who cheat, murder, and steal to get ahead. He recognized the idolatry of their self-filled lives and knew it would bring nothing but woe. In stark contrast to that misery, he declared that the glory of the Lord would fill the entire earth. And what would be Habakkuk's response to such glory? He said, "The LORD is in his holy temple; let all the earth keep silence before him" (2:20).

Habakkuk responded to God's presence with silence. Astounding. The prophet who had so much to say in the opening pages of his book is now without words. In support of Habakkuk's response, Matthew Henry commented that "It is the duty of [God's] people to attend him with silent adoring, and patiently wait for his appearing to save them in his own way and time."[2] And so Habakkuk—the prophet, the word speaker, the truth teller—is left speechless in the presence of the Lord, confident that in his own sovereign timing the Lord will save his people. It is almost as if you can feel Habakkuk exhale.

When was the last time you exhaled the craziness of life and sat before the Lord in silent adoration? Isn't it unbelievable to think that, of all we could say and do for the Lord, sometimes he just wants our silent presence with him?

> As we approach God in worship, silence
> can be more than golden. It can be the space
> we need in order to receive grace.

Being silent before God is no small challenge, I assure you. Some days I have to relentlessly pursue silence. It isn't easy. But in our silence we honor the Lord by communicating our deep trust in his will. The glory, honor, and splendor of the Lord fill every inch of space like the waters fill the sea. Silence doesn't sound like a bad idea now, does it? Are you thinking about embracing silence today too? It might be comforting to know you are in good company:

> Beginning with the Hebrews, silence has been part of our Christian tradition. Moses met God in the silence on Mt. Sinai; and Elijah discovered that God was not found in noise and activity, but in "a sound of sheer silence" (1 Kings 19:12 NRSV). Jesus, too, knew the power God found in the silence. He prepared for his ministry

in the quiet of the desert and regularly found sustenance
in quiet places where he rested in God.[3]

Moses and Elijah met God in silence. But, more importantly, if
Jesus knew to find the power of God in silence, I think the practice
is worth embracing. Especially in the progression of worship, silence
can be more than golden. It can be the space we need in order to
receive grace.

Embracing Prayer

We don't know how long Habakkuk sat silently in the presence
of the Lord. It could have been hours. Eventually, he was moved to
lift his voice, and what broke the silence was prayer. But this was
not the prayer of the wrestling prophet we saw earlier asking God,
"Why?" It was the voice of Habakkuk the embracer reaching for
God and his mercy:

> I have heard the reports about You,
>   and I am in awe when I consider all You have done.
> O Eternal One, revive Your work in our lifetime;
>   reveal it among us in our times.
> As You unleash *Your* wrath, remember *Your*
>   compassion.
>   (Habakkuk 3:1-2 THE VOICE)

This was not only a prayer; it was Habakkuk's song. Apparently
Habakkuk was quite the musician. I just love the image of him sitting in silence and having a song of prayer rise from the deepest
parts of his heart. He was moved in awe to worshipful prayer as he
remembered what God had done. Could there be anything more
beautiful?

I experienced something similar to this holy moment not too
long ago. Our church went through a massive construction project
that left us out of our worship center for months. On the first day

back in the room, our worship leading teams gathered. We began our time in silent meditation and then in corporate prayer declaring the goodness of God. As we confessed and poured out our hearts to the Lord, someone began singing. Soon a chorus of the most glorious kind was rising up. It wasn't about the talent of the singers or the beauty of the room. It was the soul-stirring presence of the Lord among us as we remembered his faithfulness to us.

Fresh-out-of-amazing vessels can be filled with
lots of things, but the only thing that will move us
toward worship is the Spirit of the living God.

For a moment, I could not bring myself to even join the song. Overwhelmed by its beauty, I fell to my knees, and all I could think of was, "Lord, you are so good to us to let us express what is in our hearts. I'm truly humbled by the opportunity to be part of what you are doing among your people." God moves into the gaps of our lives and reminds us that he is always at work. I have no idea why he chooses to allow us to join him in the work he does, but it is such a gift.

St. Augustine has been credited for saying, "He who sings, prays twice." I love the thought of Habakkuk's song being his way of praying twice. The prayer has double the significance. He was directing his praise to the Lord. As he did, the song stirred his heart to remember what the Lord had done in the days leading up to this moment. Habakkuk was also drawing close to God's heart by saying, "God, remember that you perfectly balance wrath and mercy as you deal with your people."

- Remember how you walked us out of Egypt.

- Remember how you divided the land of Canaan for your people.

- Remember how you split the waters of the Red Sea and the river Jordan.

- Remember how the sun and moon stood still when Joshua prayed.

Such remembrance of God's powerful work strengthens our faith.

As fresh-out-of-amazing girls we need to take a cue from Habakkuk and remember all that God has done in our lives. Finish this sentence: Lord, I remember how you...

Did God provide for you in the midst of a financial storm? Has he given you a true friend when you had none? Was there a moment when God called you to a new land and never once left you alone? Did he walk with you through a valley? Each of these remembrances can be your prayer to sing back to God. As a good musician builds and layers chords that move toward a glorious peak, your remembrances build and layer God's faithfulness to you over the years. Don't miss these moments, my friend. Can you feel the song rising higher and higher? We might just tremble with awe and fall silent like Habakkuk. We certainly should.

Habakkuk's reflection brought him to the end of himself, but also to complete awe of God. "He was so weak, and so unable to help himself, that he was as if rottenness had entered into his bones; he had no strength left in him, could neither stand nor go; he trembled in himself, trembled all over, trembled within him."[4] Fresh-out-of-amazing vessels can be filled with lots of things, but the only thing that will move us toward worship is the Spirit of the living God. God created our hearts to worship, and that is what Habakkuk demonstrated so well in the final verses of his song.

Embracing Worship

Habakkuk still did not have all the answers he wanted about why God was doing what he was doing. Habakkuk also knew the very real possibility that nothing would turn out how he wanted it to. So he had a decision to make:

> Would everything really be all right? Habakkuk's lip quivered a bit, and his knees trembled more than a bit. But God's unstoppable, unbeatable, unconditional love chases away all fears, and God's love made Habakkuk brave. Just like the cold can move you closer toward the fire, hard things can move you closer toward God.[5]

And what did Habakkuk do? In the face of an uncertain future, Habakkuk inhaled the breath of God and worshipped him. "While Habakkuk does not mention the Holy Spirit, there is no doubt that the Spirit was inspiring and infilling the prophet to record one of the most magnificent descriptions of Jehovah in the entire Word of God."[6] This is his song, and we can sing it too:

> Even if the fig tree does not blossom
> and there are no grapes on the vines,
> If the olive trees fail to give fruit
> and the fields produce no food,
> If the flocks die *far* from the fold
> and there are no cattle in the stalls;
> Then I will *still* rejoice in the Eternal!
> I will rejoice in the God who saves me!
> The Eternal Lord is my strength!
> He has made my feet like the feet of a deer;
> He allows me to walk on high places. (Habakkuk
> 3:17-19 The Voice)

Sometimes the bravest thing we can do is worship God. Habakkuk modeled that truth when he said, "Even if there is famine, I will still worship. Even if there is economic ruin, I will still worship. Even if it seems all hope is gone, I will still worship." Why? Because he realized that God was his true salvation and unwavering strength no matter what happened. A.W. Tozer once said, "Most of us see God too small; our God is too little. David said, 'O magnify the Lord with me,' and 'magnify' doesn't mean to make God big. You can't make God big. But you can see Him big." [7] Worship is how we see God big. Habakkuk embraced seeing God big and we can too.

Sometimes the bravest thing we can do is worship God.

What does seeing God big look like in the life of a fresh-out-of-amazing girl? We'll better answer that question once we identify our failed olive crops and empty stalls. I don't know about you, but mine looks like watching others do big things when I'm convinced my life is super small. Some days it looks like having zero answers in the parenting department or wondering how to encourage my husband when life hits hard. For the year after my father died, the vines in my life only produced a crop of bitter grapes because grief squeezed out every drop of sweet goodness. Or so I thought. Worship, as it turned out, was the key to the doorway of hope I needed to walk through. God returned my song because it was his, after all. I just needed to open my mouth and worship anyway.

She Sang There

You may recall my saying that they asked me to sing at my dad's funeral and that I couldn't do it. Well, one year to the day after his funeral, I was asked to lead worship for four services at my church.

Of course I experienced a perfect storm of emotions the entire week leading up to the weekend of worship. You might say I was a mess. I certainly would.

But the truth is, when that battle rages, we have a Savior, a Rescuer, and a Friend in Jesus. While my heart had been healing in silence and the war was raging, Jesus had been fighting for me. I have learned that Jesus never turns from us. He does not set himself at a distance from us. He enters our pain, holds us close, and moves through it with us. When Jesus walked this earth, he knew sorrow, and he was acquainted with grief. He drew near to the grieving. Ironically but wonderfully, the One who was abandoned at his most desperate hour does not abandon us in ours.

That morning as I stood to sing, I couldn't feel my legs below me. I thought for sure I was going to fall flat on the ground. Was this what Habakkuk felt when, awestruck by God's presence, he felt his strength leave him? Feeling more than a little vulnerable, I had to ask, *Lord, will I sing here?* As I stood waiting for the music to begin, my heart raced back to the day before when my worship pastor, Jon, prayed for the Lord's anointing to be upon me. I exhaled every last bit of me as well as the fears that were doing their best to keep the song buried. I breathed deep, I started singing, and I worshipped my God from the truest place of my heart.

I will tell you, I did sing that day—but I also didn't because it wasn't me singing. It was all Jesus. My patient Friend in my grief who had lifted my heart from the valley of Achor and who had walked me through the door of hope now let his song rise up out of it all. He did that for me. I'm just so humbled by his grace.

The One who was abandoned at his most desperate hour does not abandon us in ours.

Friend, I don't know where you are today, but I want to tell you from the bottom of my heart, I understand pain and grief. I also know beyond a doubt that Jesus meets us there in the wilderness. He is the Door of hope. He does not leave us—he will not leave you—alone to crumble into pieces. Jesus is with you always. He stays. He sings softly. And when your heart is ready, he gives you his song.

And then you have to decide what to do with it.

Worship Is Frontline Work

Songwriter and worship leader Martha Munizzi has this to say about wilderness times:

> God always has something he does in the wilderness. He wants to pour something into you. But, it is not just about you. It is for others, too. Worship is frontline work. It is warfare and you are leading out to sing over others who are fighting battles too.[8]

Has it ever occurred to you that your song is not meant only for you? It is so easy to be focused on our own story, isn't it? But the truth is, if we allow him, God will use our songs in the lives of others in very powerful ways. Your song, for instance, will be your declaration of his goodness despite the darkness and your absolute trust in him despite the pain. As you worship from a difficult place, others will hear your song and be reminded of important truths: "God will provide. He will not abandon me. He is good." And they will experience freedom through their faith in Jesus as the battle rages around them.

Do you know the story of King Jehoshaphat? I had forgotten it, but one of my worship pastors, Robert, referred to it to remind our choir of the power of worship. You see, when Jehoshaphat was overwhelmed by enemy attacks, he sought the Lord, and before the battle, he did something extraordinary:

> When he had taken counsel with the people, he appointed those who were to sing to the LORD and praise him in holy attire, as they went before the army, and say, "Give thanks to the LORD, for his steadfast love endures forever." And when they began to sing and praise, the LORD set an ambush against the men of Ammon, Moab, and Mount Seir, who had come against Judah, so that they were routed (2 Chronicles 20:21-22).

That's quite the battle strategy! As he marched toward the enemy, King Jehoshaphat sent out the worshippers first to give thanks to the Lord. As they began to sing, the Lord destroyed the enemy.

> As you worship from a difficult place, others will hear your song and be reminded of important truths: "God will provide. He will not abandon me. He is good." And they will experience freedom through their faith in Jesus as the battle rages around them.

We can grasp that worship pleases the heart of God, but did you know worship confuses the enemy as well? While the worshippers sang out, the Lord himself set the ambush. Your worship is like a battle cry for the Beloved to move on your behalf—and he delights in doing so. Are you encouraged by that truth today? So know that your worship is both calling on the Lord to move and act on your behalf, and reminding people around you who is on their side. Our worship is a powerful testimony to others when they see us choose worship over worry. This choice to declare praise instead of our problems also helps those around us to renew their commitment to God.

Habakkuk knew this power of worship. The final verse in chapter 3 says, "For the worship leader—a *song* accompanied by strings" (Habakkuk 3:19 THE VOICE). Habakkuk poured out a song of worship, but he didn't stop there. He then handed the music to the worship leader to use to encourage the people of God. Can you imagine when those words of prophecy Habakkuk spoke came to fruition? What hope this song would have given God's people!

Your worship is like a battle cry for the Beloved to move on your behalf—and he delights in doing so.

We, too, are the people of God, and we are still reaping the benefits of the song God put on Habakkuk's heart. God put the song on the pages of our Bible to stir up our hope and to invite us to worship no matter what is going on in our lives. Our acceptance of this invitation has ripple effects in the lives of our families, friends, brothers and sisters in our churches, and even generations to come. My sweet sister, the song you sing today has far-reaching effects. Don't ever doubt that for a minute.

Upside-Down Worship

As we close the book of Habakkuk, we are leaving him in a very different place than we found him. Hear the prophet's proclamation:

> The Eternal Lord is my strength!
> He has made my feet like the feet of a deer;
> He allows me to walk on high places (Habukkuk 3:19
>   THE VOICE).

Seeing Habukkuk walk on the high places gives us a sense of closure. But we can't forget that the way to that high place was through the lowly wrestling place of doubt and struggle. If we did not know where Habukkuk came from, the heights to which he climbed would not mean so much to us. And that is really the upside-down way of worship: to go up, we must be willing to go down. Are you familiar with this Puritan poem?

> *The Valley of Vision*
> Lord, high and holy, meek and lowly,
> Thou hast brought me to the valley of vision,
> where I live in the depths but see thee in the heights;
> hemmed in by mountains of sin I behold thy glory.
> Let me learn by paradox that the way down is the way up,
> that to be low is to be high,
> that the broken heart is the healed heart,
> that the contrite spirit is the rejoicing spirit,
> that the repenting soul is the victorious soul,
> that to have nothing is to possess all,
> that to bear the cross is to wear the crown,
> that to give is to receive,
> that the valley is the place of vision.
> Lord, in the daytime stars can be seen from deepest wells,
> and the deeper the wells the brighter thy stars shine;
> Let me find thy light in my darkness,
> thy life in my death, thy joy in my sorrow,
> thy grace in my sin,
> thy riches in my poverty thy glory in my valley. [9]

We all like the high places, don't we? Like Peter on the Mount of Transfiguration, we would like to pitch our tents and make it our home. "Lord," we ask, "can't we just stay here? This high place is really pretty awesome." But God knows that the place where we learn to look for him is in the depths. It is where broken hearts are healed, where we learn to find light in the darkness, and where, by his grace, we can know joy in our sorrow. Yes, there is a holy tension here. We come face-to-face with the reality that we will always need upside-down times and seasons when we go lower to go higher. At those times and on days when we fall short, we are more able to see God big.

We have also learned from Habakkuk that we can wrestle with God when we are in fresh-out-of-amazing places. We can toss him our doubts. We can pray through our questions. We can respond by going to our own watchpost and waiting for him to speak—because he will. And when he does, we can declare his message first to our own hearts, and then we can share it with others. We can become embracers of God who worship him, whatever this day, this moment, or this season is like, because he is worthy of our worship.

God knows that the place where we learn to look for him is in the depths of fresh out of amazing. It is where broken hearts are healed, where we learn to find light in the darkness, and where, by his grace, we can know joy in our sorrow.

In the meantime, the deeper the wells, the brighter the stars shine. So we press on. We press on to know Jesus in the depths and to worship him no matter what.

Chapter 11

P.S. Take Mercy

And so here we are. I told you we were going on a journey, and we are almost finished. But just because *we* are finished doesn't mean your journey has ended. Truthfully, I think it has only just begun.

I feel like I'm only beginning to understand that "fresh out of amazing" is where I end and where God begins. Reaching this understanding doesn't have to be a quick process. (Aren't you glad?) The important thing is that we keep moving forward, pressing on, and looking to Jesus who is "the founder and perfecter of our faith" (Hebrews 12:2).

I want to give you a gift of sorts. Only the gift is not from me. In fact, you already have everything you need to receive it for yourself. But, please, whatever you do as you put down this book, please take with you this one thing:

Please take mercy.

I don't mean cheap mercy either. The mercy I want you to grab hold of is found in one place, and it was bought with a great price.

Hebrews 4:16 instructs us to "draw near to the throne of grace, that we may receive mercy and find grace to help in time of need."

Within this verse is the most beautiful invitation for everyone who is still pondering the question we talked about in the very beginning: "Can this fresh-out-of-amazing girl live?" God *knows*. Remember? Has he revealed himself to you along the way? I promise you, he has met me in the process of writing these words. Oh, how my heart has needed them. I know I'll revisit them time and time again.

God knows our dry bones can live. He knows what we need as well as when we need it. What you and I need today is mercy. How do we get mercy? He simply says, "Come." We don't have to act a certain way or recite a specific creed to receive it. In fact, God has given us the most immediate and intimate access to mercy that we could ever ask for.

An All-Access Pass

Have you ever been backstage at a major concert or event? My friend Courtney and I had this opportunity not too long ago. She invited me to attend a *Women of Faith* event with her. I knew we had free tickets to hear some great speakers, but I had no idea we were headed backstage to visit with them. I also didn't know we would be able to stand in the wings and watch as several thousand women enjoyed a concert by Natalie Grant. It was pretty cool to be up close and personal with women I greatly respect. I was able to be backstage because one of the speakers had given us access. Afterward she said, "Come on, girls. Let's go someplace we can talk privately." When the invitation was extended, we accepted because, of course, who would say no?

Girls, we also have been extended an invitation we simply can't say no to. It is even bigger than being backstage at *Women of Faith*. Why? Because of who is inviting us and what we are being invited to: the throne of grace. God has established a way for us to meet with him. He could have chosen a thousand other ways to do it, as Matthew Henry explained:

God might have set up a tribunal of strict inexorable justice, dispensing death, the wages of sin, to all who were convened before it; but he has chosen to set up a throne of grace. A throne speaks of authority, and bespeaks awe and reverence. A throne of grace speaks great encouragement even to the chief of sinners. There grace reigns, and acts with sovereign freedom, power and bounty.[1]

The place God wants to meet us is characterized by his grace: He wants to speak encouragement to our hearts. We have access to God not because of anything we have done to deserve it. No, the reason we have been given such a sweet invitation is because of the One who sits on the throne. The One who makes this possible is our Great High Priest, Jesus, the Son of God, who "passed through the heavens *from death into new life with God*" (Hebrews 4:14 THE VOICE). But there's more:

> Jesus is not some high priest who has no sympathy for our weaknesses *and flaws*. He has already been tested in every way that we are tested; but He emerged victorious, without failing God (verse 15 THE VOICE).

Yes, Jesus conquered death and made a way for us to be in relationship with him. He also sympathizes with our weaknesses and understands our flaws, but he doesn't hang those faults over our heads and make us feel ashamed. Jesus wants us to approach him; he gives us access to his forgiveness, power, love, direction, grace, and, yes, mercy. He wholeheartedly welcomes us into his presence. And that kind of throne was unheard of in New Testament days and before.

> "Throne of grace" is an oxymoron. To the ancient world, a throne was a forbidding place of sovereign authority and judgment. If you approached a throne and the king did not hold out his scepter, you were history! You

definitely would not draw near to the throne for sympathy, especially with a trivial problem. But the author calls it the throne of *grace*. He makes it clear that we are welcome at this throne.[2]

The writer of Hebrews might as well be saying, "Hey fresh-out-of-amazing girl, you are welcome here." Do you know what being "welcome at this throne" of God means? We can bring our burdens and busyness, we can lay down our shattered dreams, we can tell God we have never felt amazing, we can pour out all the lies our hearts have been believing, and we can certainly cry the bitter tears stored up in our grieving hearts. Friend, simply put, it is good for us to approach the throne of grace.

I could sit with that truth for days—and that's not yet the complete picture. It is good to have access to the throne, but it is even better because Jesus is the One sitting there and doing the inviting. And He tells us the way to approach his throne of grace. He doesn't tell us to come meekly. He doesn't point to us with his nail-scarred hand and say, "Hang your head, you sinner." No, Jesus tells us to approach him with *fearless confidence*—and that truth astounds me. When I am fresh out of amazing, I do not feel bold. Hardly! I want to run *away from* everything, not *to* anything. I want to hide. But this passage says to step boldly. I want to be a girl who has fearless confidence, don't you? I want to know the heart of the One who can give me what my heart needs.

Still, some of us might be a little bit hindered in our understanding of the significance of approaching a throne. We don't understand monarchy and tradition like those who have grown up in a country where princes and princesses grow up to be kings and queens. When you go to London, England, for example, you can't march into Buckingham Palace, past the guard gate, and yell, "Hey! It's okay! The queen has given me access." Procedures and protocols are in place to keep common people out of the presence of the queen.

We can relate in some small degree to trying to get an audience with the president of the United States. Though he resides at what we call "The People's House," we can't drop in for a visit anytime we like. It just isn't permitted.

There is an exception to this inaccessibility of our presidents, however. If you get to Maranatha Baptist Church in Plains, Georgia, early enough on Saturday night and are willing to sleep in your car, you can listen to the thirty-ninth president of the United States teach a Sunday school lesson the next morning. President Jimmy Carter has been teaching at this small Baptist church for years. He has always drawn a steady crowd, but the numbers grew considerably after he was diagnosed with brain cancer. Still, if you want to have immediate access to someone who once held the most important office in America, the former president of the United States is relatively accessible at Maranatha Baptist Church. The rules are pretty simple, and they are stated to all visitors:

> No one would interrupt the lesson by taking photos.
> The president. Did not. Do selfies.
> Everyone would get a picture with Rosalynn and
> Jimmy, but no one would hug or kiss him, because no
> one wanted him to get sick.
> And don't say, "Oh, I'm so sorry about the diagnosis"…You don't have to tell him. He knows it. Just say,
> "I'm praying for you."
> More rules: There would be no applause for the former
> president. No one would stand when he entered. As
> a result, Carter slipped into the room at 10 a.m. sharp,
> with no fanfare.[3]

When I read this article about President Jimmy Carter, I was so touched by his humility. He does not demand fanfare, though he certainly could. Instead, he chooses to share truths from the Word of God.

I can't help but see Jesus in the way President Carter interacts with normal, everyday Americans who show up to hear him teach. Jesus deserves all of the fanfare we could muster up. He sits on the throne because he is worthy. But, more than he wants our applause, he wants our hearts. Jesus says, "Come. Be near the throne of grace. Be near me." Where else can we go and be "kindly invited to the mercy-seat, where grace reigns, and loves to exert and exalt itself toward us"?[4] Oh girls, we really should be found in this grace place.

What We Need

What is it that we honestly need? Oh, we might say we need a Diet Coke, thinner legs, or a maid to come to our house once a week. It would be awesome if my girls would do the dishes on their own and dinner would magically arrive on the table each night. Those would all make my life easier. But if I answer this question from the deepest part of my heart, I know that I need the brand-new-every-morning mercy of Jesus to meet me at the start of a day. Luckily God has said something about this already:

> The steadfast love of the LORD never ceases;
>> his mercies never come to an end;
> they are new every morning;
>> great is your faithfulness.
> "The LORD is my portion, " says my soul,
>> "therefore I will hope in him" (Lamentations 3:22-24).

God offers a fresh new batch of mercy every morning. Even before your coffeepot finishes brewing, God's mercy is ready and waiting for you.

And what exactly is mercy? It is simply God's "kindness or good will towards the miserable and the afflicted, joined with a desire to help them."[5] God's mercy is evidence in how he treats us when we are fresh out of amazing. And mercy is what we need when our hearts are broken, hurting, and weary. The wording of this

Lamentations passage in the original Hebrew says that because of God's mercy, we are not "consumed, exhausted, spent, or finished."[6] Mercy bends his heart toward us with a holy influence that will guard and strengthen our faith.

> Even before your coffeepot finishes brewing,
> God's mercy is ready and waiting for you.

When we feel finished, God desires to help us. He knew from the start we would need it. He has provided and continues to provide us with help because his mercies never come to an end. Or, to put it another way, when we are exhausted, God's mercies are not. They are fresh every morning. And guess what, friends? It is always morning somewhere. So receive the mercy you need today—and know that your need can't deplete the gift.

The invitation here is simply to come to the throne of grace and receive what we need. Of course, it's hard to receive anything before you are fresh out of amazing. If you don't have a need, you won't come. But when you are emptied, when you're aware of all the places you're lacking, when you're weak and weary, you can more easily give yourself permission to come. And you need to come.

Aligning my life with this truth looks like the act of coming to God's throne and receiving his grace. I need to plant myself front and center at the throne of grace and gaze upon Jesus. It is a habit I am slowly learning. I'm so grateful he is a gentle and patient teacher.

When You Need It

Ideally, we would be in the habit of daily approaching our Lord's throne and receiving his mercies before we are in a critical place of need. It makes sense, doesn't it? But if you are like me, you tend to live in survival mode most days. Trust me, I understand more than you know. For example, it makes total sense that I would bulk order things my family of six needs regularly, like toilet paper. I don't plan on running out, but inevitably I am found rushing to the grocery store seven minutes before they close because we are down to one precious roll. I find myself wondering how in the world we could exhaust our supply when I just bought some last week. Of course, when we have a need, I go to the place I know I can fill it. I'm a rock-star mom like that. Never mind I huff and puff all the way to the store. I'm working on that, I promise.

> God's mercy is our manna,
> and we are to gather it daily.

But God knows how we are. It isn't like he hasn't been through this before with his people. Remember the nation of Israel wandering in the desert demanding food? In order to teach them to trust him, God allowed them to hunger. I wrote about this in *Hope for the Weary Mom*:

> "Tell them, 'In the evening, you will have meat to eat; and in the morning you will have enough bread to satisfy your gnawing hunger. Then you will know that I am the Eternal your God'" (Exodus 16:12 THE VOICE).
>
> I think he allowed [his chosen people] to feel real hunger so he could feed them and be their provision. He wanted to be their source. Daily they gathered bread and meat and were fed by their God.

Don't we do the same thing, friend? We are hungry and so we complain. But we need him to fill our hearts, not our stomachs. We say things like "I'm here and I'm dying, Lord. I can't take another step in this journey...Where is my bread?"

"I am the bread of life" (John 6:48). There is no doubt that he is the soul food we need in the middle of our weariness. Just like the Israelites gathered enough manna for each day, we too need to gather from God's Word daily. He wants to be our source [of life] as well.[7]

God's mercy is our manna today, and we are to gather it daily. After all, is there ever a time we don't need it? But as we said before, we often wait until our survival depends on it.

Could you use some help today? Maybe you need it in the worst way. Maybe you feel like your life is falling apart. Maybe your need is a deep, deep well. So, in times like that, what does God's help look like?

Help: is a technical nautical term that is used elsewhere only in Acts 27:17 to describe the cables that the sailors wrapped around the hull of Paul's ship during the storm so that it would not break apart.[8]

Picture this with me. When life is wrecked by storms and we feel like we are breaking apart, God wraps us in his tender mercy and grace. He holds us together by his great and unfailing new-every-morning mercies. So, is your life coming apart? Draw near to the throne of grace for the help you need to hold yourself together. Take the mercy, dear friend. But don't stop there.

Live Mercy, Give Mercy

As you look around, I wonder if you can see anyone else whose life might be coming apart and who would benefit from a little mercy talk. I think it is safe to say you and I aren't the only ones who have ever felt fresh out of amazing. Having journeyed together thus far, you and I may just have something to give to others we meet along the way.

We need to live mercy, and then we need to give mercy.

You see, we understand that because of our sin and brokenness, God could choose to leave us as we are. But he does not. Why? Titus 3:3-8 tells us...

> There was a time when we, too, were foolish, rebellious, and deceived—we were slaves to sensual cravings and pleasures; and we spent our lives being spiteful, envious, hated by many, and hating one another. But then *something happened*: God our Savior and His overpowering love and kindness for humankind entered our world; He came to save us. It's not that *we earned it* by doing good works or righteous deeds; He came because He is merciful. He brought us *out of our old ways of living* to a new beginning through the washing of regeneration; and He made us completely new through the Holy Spirit, who was poured out in abundance through Jesus the Anointed, our Savior. *All of this happened* so that through His grace we would be accepted *into God's covenant family* and appointed to be His heirs, full of the hope that comes from *knowing you have* eternal life. This is a faithful statement *of what we believe* (The Voice).

It is because of God's mercy that he saved us from the consequences and darkness of our sin in the first place. He has brought us out of our old ways of living, washed us, and made us new because he is the God of mercy. The word *regeneration* here is an "amen" word if I ever saw it. (What is an "amen" word? It is the type of word that makes someone in the back row of the church shout "Amen!" on Sunday morning.) Why? What does it mean? I love this from Raechel Myers of *She Reads Truth*:

> The word he uses is "regeneration." In Latin it means "to create again" and in Greek it's *paliggenesía* or "birth, beginning." The washing of regeneration Paul describes is a complete cleaning in which our filth becomes a distant memory and we as believers are literally a *New Creation*.[9]

The truth is evident—once we were rebellious and deceived by sin. God in his great mercy "created us again" by washing us clean. We are made new by his Spirit because of the life, death, and resurrection of Jesus Christ. He saved us because of his overpowering love and kindness. It was his mercy. Amen? Yes. Amen.

But for some reason, we too often receive the salvation mercy and then quickly leave it behind because, of course, we think we need to be amazing on our own merit. We know all about merit, don't we? We have already covered at length why that doesn't work.

And then, on other days we don't feel very "regenerated," do we? We come face-to-face with the reality of our sins on a daily basis and we wonder why God bothers with us. *Did you yell at your kids today? Maybe someone cut you off in traffic and you gave a few driving pointers, loudly for all to hear. Or, perhaps, let's just say you told your husband a thing or two that has been on your mind for about six weeks. Maybe you didn't say it with one ounce of grace.* As a result sin shows up and tells us who we once were and we begin to revert back to our old ways. We forget we are "created new." Girls, we don't have to do that anymore. We get to live mercy knowing full well we don't deserve any of it. Take a look back at the verses in Titus. What do you see?

His overpowering love and kindness.

He came to save us.

He came because he is merciful.

He brought us *out of our old ways of living* to a new beginning.

He made us completely new through the Holy Spirit

> ...who was poured out in abundance through Jesus the Anointed, our Savior.

This mercy living is everyday gospel living and we should remind ourselves of it daily. His rich mercy and great love is not wishful thinking. It is truth for your heart and mine. We can't earn it and we can't lose it because every bit of it starts with God. Seriously, with such sweet news we can't keep this to ourselves. We need to live mercy, and then we need to give mercy.

Recently I was rereading an old favorite, *Abba's Child* by Brennan Manning. In the chapter "Come Out of Hiding," he wrote this:

> Christians who remain in hiding continue to live the lie. We deny the reality of our sin. In a futile attempt to erase our past, we deprive the community of our healing gift. If we conceal our wounds out of fear and shame, our inner darkness can neither be illuminated nor become a light for others.[10]

Fresh Out of Amazing is my come-out-of-hiding story. I don't want to conceal my wounds anymore. I'm inviting the light of the gospel of Jesus into this place once and for all. I'm praying that this message lights the way for others so they can come out of hiding too. I am finally at a place in my life where I want to shout from the rooftops, "If you see anything in me that looks like a hint of amazing, it is all Jesus. From beginning to end he is the only one who is amazing." This imagined holler echoes what I learned last year from the book of 1 John:

> We want to tell you about the One who was from the beginning. We have seen Him with our own eyes, heard

Him with our own ears, and touched Him with our own hands. This One is *the manifestation of* the life-giving Voice, and He showed us real life, *eternal life.* We have seen it *all, and we can't keep what* we witnessed *quiet*— we have to share it with you. *We are inviting you to experience* eternal life through the One who was with the Father and came down to us. What we saw and heard we pass on to you so that you, too, will be connected with us intimately *and become family.* Our family is united by our connection with the Father and His Son Jesus, the Anointed One; and we write all this because retelling this story fulfills our joy.

What we are telling you now is the very message we heard from Him: God is *pure* light, undimmed by darkness of any kind (1 John 1:1-5 THE VOICE).

So this is real-light mercy living. It is the light of the gospel that displaces fear and shame. We have experienced it. We have seen with our own eyes what God can do in the hearts of his daughters when we draw near him. We simply can't keep quiet about the work he has done and is doing in our lives. Why wouldn't I want to share it with others? Why wouldn't you? When we tell our stories, we are able to connect deeply with others in Christ, and our stories can bring joy and hope to those who hear them. At the same time, we reap the benefits of joy and hope as, in telling our stories, we review God's goodness and faithfulness to us.

If you see anything in me that looks like a hint of amazing, it is all Jesus. From beginning to end he is the only One who is amazing.

Not too long ago I wore my favorite cross necklace to church on Sunday morning. This was not just any cross necklace, mind you. It was handmade by my dear friend Lori.[11] I don't know how she does it, but she has the ability to marry the classic beauty of a strand of pearls with the rustic charm of a vintage metal cross. It is the perfect combination, and without exception, whenever I wear it, women always ask me where they can find one too. I am happy to point them to Lori's website, so I pretty much have my sales pitch ready whenever I wear it. I love supporting home businesses, and of course Lori is so talented.

On this morning, I had already shared with a couple women about the cross and where they could find it. Still, as I was coming out of church, I was not surprised when I was stopped in the crowd, and a woman commented on it. But it was how she spoke that grabbed my heart. With her eyes fixed completely on the cross, she said half to herself and half to me, "Oh, that cross is so beautiful." I smiled and gave her my standard response of how Lori made it and where to find it. Still looking at the cross but making a mental note, she said, "Okay! I'm going to get one when I can." She then went on to tell me she was living in a home associated with our church for women transitioning out of a correctional facility. "As soon as I have transitioned out, I'm going to buy one," she told me. "I just love it so much."

I was overcome with emotion. I understood what it meant for this precious woman to be standing there. Mercy had made it possible for her to be walking into church and moving forward in her life, not backward. More importantly I saw in her eyes the sweetest love for the cross of Jesus that I have ever seen. I hugged her and said with tears in my own eyes, "Oh! I'm so glad you are here today!" As my arms went around her neck, the Lord spoke swiftly and distinctly: "Give her this one. Give her your cross." As I was letting go of her, I reached around my neck, took off my cross in one swoop, and put it around her neck.

*The gospel multiplied is more astounding than
I can express. It is worth my life, my all.*

"Here, I want you to have this one." Immediately her hand went to her mouth, and she began to weep, trying to protest the gift. But there was no way I was not going to share this with her. Do you know why? God wanted her to have this as a sweet sign of how much he loved her. Giving my favorite cross to this precious woman brought me so much joy. In fact, giving her the cross made my joy in the beautiful necklace complete.

Finally, why are we surprised that God's invitation to see him big would include us sharing his bigness—his big mercy, his big love—with others? Sharing the truth of his love—the truth that sets people free—has always been his heart, and that purpose needs to become ours as well. The beautiful part is that fresh-out-of-amazing girls are not exempt from obeying God's call and sharing it. The invitation to give to others the mercy we ourselves have lived helps our wounds heal too. The gospel multiplied is more astounding than I can express. It is worth my life, my all.

Mercy Is the Theme of Our Song

I came across an old hymn, and I can't help but think this is the perfect way to offer a blessing for your heart today. I didn't write these words, but I've been singing them since I found them. Should our paths ever cross in this world, more than on the pages of this book, I pray you will hear me singing the song of God's great mercy. I'd be so humbled to hear you join me. And, really, it just seems fitting for us to end this chapter—this book—with a song, doesn't it?

Thy mercy, my God is the theme of my song,
The joy of my heart and the boast of my tongue;
Thy free grace alone, from the first to the last,
Hath won my affections and bound my soul fast.

Without thy free mercy I could not live here;
Sin soon would reduce me to utter despair;
But, through thy free goodness, my spirits revive,
And he that first made me, still keeps me alive.

Thy mercy surpasses the sin of my heart
Which wonders to feel its own hardness depart,
Dissolved by thy goodness, I fall to the ground
And weep to the praise of the mercy I found.

Thy mercy in Jesus exempts me from hell;
Its glories I'll sing, and its wonders I'll tell:
'Twas Jesus the friend when he hung on the tree
That opened the channel of mercy for me.

Great Father of mercies, thy goodness I own,
And covenant love of thy crucified son:
All praise to the spirit, whose action divine
Seals mercy and pardon and righteousness mine.[12]

Afterword

I love it when a story lets you peek into the "and they lived happily ever after" part. After all, even when we close the book, the characters continue to live on in our hearts and minds. We are desperate to know what comes next, aren't we?

What happens next for us? What does our epilogue say? Where do we go from here? I believe what happens next is very important. *Fresh Out of Amazing* has not simply been a book project for me. It has begun a healing work in my life. One reason is that I have planted myself with both feet in the Word of God. As Bible teacher Priscilla Shirer said, "The one place you can be absolutely sure Jesus will show up is in the pages of God's Word." Simply put, Jesus has shown up, he brought healing to my heart, and I am not one bit surprised.

When I look back over my life, every time I have found myself in a deep, deep pit, the one thing that made it possible for me to climb out was the Word of God. I take great comfort in the promise of Isaiah 40:8—"The grass withers, the flower fades, but the word of our God will stand forever." God's Word will not wither even if I feel like I might. And when my heart would rather fade into the background, God is just getting started. His Word is perpetual, unending, and continuous. So is the healing he wants to bring into my life and yours. Life lived with and for Jesus really does just keep getting better.

I've decided what happens next in my journey—or maybe I should say where I go next. I'm going to Capernaum. I know what you are thinking: "Capernaum? That came out of left field. I really thought you were going to say Starbucks or maybe Disney World. Why Capernaum?" I'm so glad you asked.

What is so special about Capernaum? Located by the Sea of Galilee, Capernaum[1] was the place Jesus moved right after he stood strong against Satan's temptations. This flourishing town was Jesus's town of choice. You see, Capernaum was a popular destination along the Via Marias, an international highway that ran from Syria to Egypt. Any news that came out of Capernaum could travel fast in both directions. Crowds gathered in this fishing town; some came by land and others by sea. The important point is they came to Capernaum by droves. There they could buy fish and other goods, and they could visit the local synagogue.

Of course Capernaum was crawling with fishermen. Jesus changed the lives of four named Peter, James, Andrew, and John when, on the shores of Capernaum, he said, "Come and follow me, and I will make you fishers of men." Here in Capernaum Jesus built his ministry; here in Capernaum his first disciples believed—and their lives were never the same. And here in Capernaum...

- Jesus probably lived in Peter's home.
- Jesus preached the Word of God daily in the synagogue.
- Jesus performed many miracles, including healing the paralytic and the centurion's servant.
- People searched for Jesus, sometimes by boat.
- Those with eyes of faith saw the Worthy One.

But nothing Jesus did was ever simply by chance. Everything he did had a divine purpose. The choice of Capernaum was not only strategic for his ministry, but it was the fulfillment of an ancient prophecy:

There will be no gloom for her who was in anguish. In the former time [the Lord] brought into contempt the land of Zebulun and the land of Naphtali, but in the latter time he has made glorious the way of the sea, the land beyond the Jordan, Galilee of the nations (Isaiah 9:1).

Capernaum was the land between Zebulun and Naphtali, and Jesus's presence there made it glorious. It was a time and place where God's people hadn't "seen a hint of light or hope of day,"[2] and God did something new.

I am longing for God to do something new in my life, and that kind of work begins with the soul-stirring presence of Jesus. I'm not actually going to Capernaum, although a girl can dream. Capernaum, to me, has become a fascinating image of the place I want to be spiritually, a place where I can...

- Seek Jesus
- Grow my faith
- Hear God's Word
- Respond to Jesus's calling to follow him
- Experience God's healing
- Get counsel for decisions

To put it in simple terms, my heart longs to go to Capernaum. I want to sit at the feet of Jesus and learn from him.

I am longing for God to do something new in my life, and that kind of work begins with the soul-stirring presence of Jesus.

That said, may I toss one more invitation your way? (You saw it coming, right?) This invitation is open-ended, and it has absolutely nothing to do with my book. It has to do with another book—the Bible. God's Word is living and active. It will stir your fresh-out-of-amazing heart like nothing else can. My heartfelt prayer is that this book, this small offering, makes you want to grab your Bible and get to know better the Great Big God who desires to revive your heart. That is exactly what Jesus has done for this fresh-out-of-amazing girl. I know he will do it for you too.

Wanting my life to be purposeful and strategic as I move on from here, I'm running full force to the feet of Jesus. And if Jesus in his sweet mercy adds a touch of the glorious (I have a feeling he just might), well, I'll be more than okay with that. As we gather in our own Capernaum places, may we look forward and may our epilogues each read like this:

> Since we [fresh-out-of-amazing girls] stand surrounded by *all those who have gone before,* an enormous cloud of witnesses, let us drop every extra weight, every sin that clings to us *and slackens our pace,* and let us run with endurance the long race set before us. Now stay focused on Jesus, who designed and perfected our faith. He endured the cross and ignored the shame *of that death* because He focused on the joy that was set before Him; and now He is seated beside God on the throne, *a place of honor* (Hebrews 12:1-2 THE VOICE).

And to God be the glory!

The LOL Mini-Challenge

*T*his is a seven-day challenge you can start today. This should only take a few minutes a day except for the final day. Invite a friend to join you.

Day 1: Read 1 John 4:18. Ask God to let his love be well formed in you.

Day 2: Write 1 John 4:18 in your journal and then a prayer that reflects your heart.

Day 3: Rewrite 1 John 4:18 in your own words. Disengage from the noise of the world for several minutes, if not an hour or more.

Day 4: Read Proverbs 31:25. Ask God to clothe you in "strength and dignity."

Day 5: Write Proverbs 31:25 in your journal and a prayer that reflects your heart.

Day 6: Rewrite Proverbs 31:25 in your journal. Engage your heart with God by taking time for some personal worship.

Day 7: Read 1 John 4:18 and Proverbs 31:25 in a different translation than you've used this week. Pray. Get together with your LOL challenge partner for coffee or lunch and share the ways God met you during your week. Challenge each other to memorize one or both of these verses.

When your week is complete, find another verse to focus on or memorize for the next week. Be sure to hold each other accountable in the days ahead. You can even set another coffee date in the future to make sure you continue to connect.

Bonus: Each of you can invite one friend to join you for a second week of the LOL Mini-Challenge. Explain the concept of *Living Loved, Only One Audience Member Matters,* and *Looking to Connect, Not Compare.* You can repeat the entire process again, or you can choose two new verses that focus on God's love and our calling as women of faith. You can let your group grow by twos each week, or you might choose to cap it off at four, six, or eight members. Whatever works for you and your community is fine. As time passes and relationships deepen, move on to reading and studying a book of the Bible. The key is to keep moving forward...together.

Study Guide for Small Groups

One of my favorite things in life is gathering a small group of women together to dive deep into heart-to-heart conversations. Not too long ago I took part in such a group. We focused on God's Word but also read books that went along with what we were studying in Scripture. Our meetings proved to be some of the sweetest times I have spent around a table as we shared honestly about life, grew in our faith, and prayed for one another. I would be crazy honored if you chose to do something similar with *Fresh Out of Amazing*. I think it has the potential to connect the hearts of women in an authentic way. Might I make a couple gentle suggestions if you are planning to embark on a small-group study?

1. Ground the study in God's Word. Each chapter has verses and stories you can find in your Bible. Take your Bible with you each week. Pick a section of Scripture to read aloud with your group. Then let God's living and active Word do its work in yielded hearts and open minds.

2. As the leader, bathe your group in prayer. Start now: Ask God to lead you to the women he wants you to invite. Pray as you read through the book and highlight discussion points. Pray when you gather. Be committed

to praying for one another between meetings. Begin and
end your time with prayer.

3. Find a co-leader. Do not attempt to lead a group of
women alone. God made us to need one another in the
most beautiful way. I find if you lead one week and she
leads the next week, you will have a chance to sit back
and minister in an entirely different way. Also, you
might invite a third person to be hostess. Find someone
who has the gift of hospitality, and her gifts will shine
as women are offered coffee and treats during your time
together. Having a hostess will bless the women who
attend and bless you.

4. Plan to meet for no more than six or seven weeks. (I
find it a blessing to let women know how many weeks
are involved so they can arrange their schedules to be
present. Most women could join you for six nights of
discussion.) This book has eleven chapters. You can
easily meet one time to get to know one another, and
then cover about two chapters each week for five or six
weeks. When you are finished, you might decide to take
a break or pick another book.

5. Each chapter in the small-group study guide follows
the same format: *encouragement* for your heart from
God's Word; *connection* through discussion; and *growth*
with life application. I find it is also a good idea to have
women highlight the three or four statements in each
chapter that are most significant to them. They should
be prepared to share one of their favorites and why it
spoke to them.

6. Do me a favor, please. Email me at stacey@staceythacker.
com and let me know your group is meeting. I'd love to
pray for you and answer any questions you might have.

Chapter 1
Can This Fresh-Out-of-Amazing Girl Live?

Encouragement: Ezekiel 37:1-14

Connection:

1. Share the statement from chapter 1 that was most significant to you and explain why it spoke to your heart.

2. What in your life does God want to resurrect, restore, and renew?

3. Can you, a fresh-out-of-amazing girl, live? What can God *not* do?

Growth:

1. Write out your own prayer of commitment to the Lord.

2. Memorize and Share: "He who began a good work in you will bring it to completion at the day of Jesus Christ" (Philippians 1:6). Be ready to say it aloud during next week's group discussion. I find that when you know you have to recite a verse to the group, memorizing becomes a higher priority. Also, as you memorize verses together, they become even more meaningful. So try to relax. I assure you the others will cheer you on and even help you if you suddenly forget and are completely wordless!

Chapter 2
Burdened and Busy

Encouragement: Luke 10:38-42

Connection:

1. Share the statement from chapter 2 that was most significant to you and explain why it spoke to your heart.

2. Why has being responsible left you burdened, busy, and quite possibly bossy?

3. What part of Martha's story grabs your heart the most?

Growth:

1. What do you need to tell Jesus right now?

2. Memorize and Share: "Are you tired? Worn out? Burned out on religion? Come to me. Get away with me and you'll recover your life. I'll show you how to take a real rest. Walk with me and work with me—watch how I do it. Learn the unforced rhythms of grace. I won't lay anything heavy or ill-fitting on you. Keep company with me and you'll learn to live freely and lightly" (Matthew 11:28-30 MSG). I realize this is a lengthy passage. You can choose to work on it slowly or just memorize the first few lines. Oh, but you will reap so many benefits if you commit to memorizing the whole thing! I promise!

Chapter 3
She's Amazing and I'm Not

Encouragement: Genesis 29:16-23

Connection:

1. Share the statement from this chapter that was most significant to you and explain why.

2. Which sister do you find yourself identifying with more, Rachel or Leah? Why?

3. Who is one woman you would like to imitate free from the curse of comparison? List two to three characteristics she displays that you want to see in your own life.

Growth:

1. Memorize and Share: "Be strong and courageous. Do not be frightened, and do not be dismayed, for the LORD your God is with you wherever you go" (Joshua 1:9).

2. This week disengage from one thing that might be leading you to compare yourself to others.

3. While you are disengaging from that one thing, focus your heart on the One who is sovereign by praying and meditating on his Word. At the end of the week, note the ways he spoke to you and what he said.

Chapter 4
I Feel Like My Dreams Have Died

Encouragement: 1 Samuel 1:1-20

Connection:

1. Share the statement from this chapter that was most significant to you and explain why.

2. Are you "barren" yet "still believing," friend? Be brave and share your story.

3. Be honest with yourself: have anger and bitterness moved into your heart? If not now, has this been true of you in the past? What about Hannah's faith fuels your faith?

Growth:

1. Memorize and Share: "My soul quietly waits for the True God alone because I hope only in Him" (Psalm 62:5 THE VOICE).

2. List examples of God's faithfulness to you in the past. May it prompt a joyous and faith-filled cry of heartfelt gratitude.

Chapter 5
Liar, Liar, Pants on Fire

Encouragement: John 4:1-40

Connection:

1. Share the statement from chapter 5 that was most significant to you and explain why.

2. What have the lying dragons in your life been telling you lately?

3. Which of the four truths played out in Jesus's conversation with the woman at the well do you most struggle to believe? Why?

Growth:

1. Memorize and Share: "We are demolishing arguments and ideas, every high-and-mighty philosophy that pits itself against the knowledge of *the one true* God. We are taking prisoners of every thought, *every emotion*, and subduing them into obedience to the Anointed One" (2 Corinthians 10:5 The Voice).

2. Learn the ABCs of slaying your lying dragons—and then make the time to do so. The harvest will be worth it!

Chapter 6
When You've Lost Your Song in the Valley of Bitterness

Encouragement: Hosea 2:14-15

Connection:

1. Share the statement from this chapter that was most significant to you and explain why.

2. What loss or painful experience prompted a season of grief in your life? If you are able to, talk about that time in your life.

3. In what ways did God provide for Naomi during her own valley of bitterness? What similar provisions did he make for you? What different provisions?

Growth:

1. Memorize and Share: "[Jesus] is before all things, and in him all things hold together" (Colossians 1:17).

2. Stories like Naomi's can make us want to look the other way. But in what way, if at all, do you see yourself in her and/or in her story? In prayer and by faith, release that part of your heart to the God of hope who is not finished with you yet.

3. The invitation to see God big is an invitation to all fresh-out-of-amazing girls no matter how they arrived at this place. Are you ready to move forward and look at life through eyes of faith? Take some time this week to reflect on how you ran out of amazing and where you are headed now.

Chapter 7
Wrestling

Encouragement: Habakkuk 1:1-2,5,12-13

Connection:

1. Share the statement from this chapter that was most significant to you and explain why.

2. What kind of wrestler are you?

3. In what ways, if any, does surrender feel like weakness to you? Why?

Growth:

1. Memorize and Share: "You did not receive the spirit of slavery to fall back into fear, but you have received the Spirit of adoption as sons, by whom we cry, 'Abba! Father!' The Spirit himself bears witness with our spirit that we are children of God" (Romans 8:15-16).

2. Reflect on what Habakkuk 1 teaches about who God is.

   a. Everlasting (1:12)

   b. Holy (1:12)

   c. The Rock (1:12)

   d. "You who are of purer eyes" (1:13)

   e. Creator (1:14)

3. What is the *shava* or cry of your heart today? Journal your thoughts and let God lead you in a prayer of surrender.

Chapter 8
Watch and Wait

Encouragement: Habakkuk 2:1-3

Connection:

1. Share the statement from chapter 8 that was most significant to you and explain why.

2. Have you had a defining moment in your life when you were willing to stop wrestling and instead watch and wait for the Lord to act or to direct you? Tell the group about that time.

3. Identify what you need most right now and explain why: perspective (to see God); positioning (to hear from God); or patience (to build endurance).

Growth:

1. Memorize and share: "Behold, I am doing a new thing; now it springs forth, do you not perceive it? I will make a way in the wilderness and rivers in the desert" (Isaiah 43:19).

2. Push the pause button this week for however long you are able. During that time, take stock of your life and/or spend time cultivating your love relationship with the Lord.

Chapter 9
Write It Down

Encouragement: Habakkuk 2:2-4

Connection:

1. Share the statement from this chapter that was most significant to you and explain why.

2. Do you consider yourself a writer? Why or why not?

3. Which is easier for you: *savoring* words or *saying* words? Why do you think that is? In what way can you use that preference in ministry?

Growth:

1. Memorize and Share: "You are our letter, every word burned onto our hearts to be read by everyone. You are the living letter of the Anointed One, *the Liberating King,* nurtured by us and inscribed, not with ink, but with the Spirit of the living God—*a letter too passionate* to be chiseled onto stone tablets, but *emblazoned* upon the human heart" (2 Corinthians 3:2-3 THE VOICE).

2. Someone once said it takes twenty-one days to form a habit. Will you accept the challenge to journal for the next three weeks and see what God does in the quietness of your heart and on the page as you preach the gospel to yourself daily?

3. Make time to write encouraging words to others. Write a note, post it on their Facebook wall, or tell them in person over a cup of coffee.

Chapter 10
Worship: Even If...I Still Will

Encouragement: Habakkuk 3:17-19

Connection:

1. Share the statement from chapter 10 that was most significant to you and explain why.

2. Finish this statement, "Lord, I remember how you..."

3. God has been working in you during this fresh-out-of-amazing season. Describe how you see him at work.

Growth:

1. Memorize and Share: "Yet I will rejoice in the LORD; I will take joy in the God of my salvation. GOD, the Lord, is my strength; he makes my feet like the deer's; he makes me tread on my high places" (Habakkuk 3:18-19).

2. What are your failed olive crops and empty stalls? Name them and, by faith, give them over to God in prayer.

3. The heartfelt worship you choose to do in this fresh-out-of-amazing place is not only for you. People who notice your worship will be encouraged to trust God and, whatever is going on in their lives, join you in worshipping him. Of the people you know, who might need to hear your song of praise? Pray that God will soon give you the chance to declare his goodness and thereby give them hope.

Chapter 11
P.S. Take Mercy

Encouragement: Hebrews 4:14-16

Connection:

1. Share the statement from this chapter that was most significant to you and explain why.

2. What keeps you from approaching the throne of grace more regularly? More expectantly? More confidently?

3. Even as God in his mercy is healing our hearts, we are to extend mercy to others. Identify one way you can give mercy today or tell about a time you desperately needed mercy and received that gift.

Growth:

1. Memorize and Share: "The steadfast love of the LORD never ceases; his mercies never come to an end; they are new every morning; great is your faithfulness. 'The LORD is my portion,' says my soul, 'therefore I will hope in him'" (Lamentations 3:22-24).

2. God's mercy is your manna. So make a plan to gather it daily from his Word. Will you meet with him in the morning? During your lunch break? While you commute to work or the kids are napping? Make a plan and stick to it.

3. Think about telling your own story. In light of the work God has done and is doing in our lives, we simply can't keep quiet! Besides, why wouldn't we want to share it with others? Remember, by retelling our stories we are able to connect deeply with others in Christ, and

those connections bring joy to us as we share and to those who hear. If you do share your story, I'd love to hear about it. Please email me at stacey@staceythacker.com and tell me how God used or is using your broken places for his glory. Let him shine bright through you. I promise he will.

Notes

Chapter 1

1. Stacey Thacker, "Steve Jobs, Me, and Being Fresh Out of Amazing," stacey thacker.com (blog), August 25, 2011, http://staceythacker.com/steve-jobs -me-and-being-fresh-out-of-amazing.

2. "Prophesy" Blue Letter Bible, accessed May 27, 2015, http://www.blueletter -bible.org.

3. "Hope"(*tiqvah*), Blue Letter Bible, accessed May 20, 2015.

4. Kristene DiMarco, "Believing What You're Singing," WORSHIP U, accessed May 28, 2015, http://www.worshipu.com/blog/believing-what-youre-singing -kristene-dimarco/.

5. Matthew Henry, *Matthew Henry's Commentary on the Bible*, Bible Gateway, accessed November 17, 2014, https://www.biblegateway.com/resources/ matthew-henry/toc.

6. Billy Graham, *Quotes from Billy Graham: A Legacy of Faith* (Nashville, TN: B&H Publishing Group, 2013).

Chapter 2

1. Tom Rath, *StrengthsFinder 2.0* (New York: Gallup Press, 2007), 149.

2. Ibid.

3. Kevin DeYoung, *Crazy Busy: A (Mercifully) Short Book About a (Really) Big Problem* (Wheaton, IL: Crossway, 2013), 49.

4. Matthew Henry, *Matthew Henry's Commentary on the Bible*, accessed May 28, 2015.

5. J.H. Hall, *Biography of Gospel Song and Hymn Writers* (New York: Fleming H. Revell, 1914).

6. Elisha A. Hoffman, "I Must Tell Jesus," *Select Hymns* (Anderson, IN: The Gospel Trumpet Company, 1911), 427.

Chapter 3

1. "Chapter 13," *The Voyage of the Dawn Treader*, directed by Michael Apted (20th Century Fox, 2010), DVD.

2. Sally Lloyd-Jones, *The Jesus Storybook Bible: Every Story Whispers His Name* (Grand Rapids, MI: Zondervan, 2007), 74.

3. Sara Hagerty, "A Call from (and to) the Hurting Before Mother's Day," Every Bitter Thing Is Sweet (blog), May 6, 2015, http://everybitterthingissweet.com/2015/05/a-call-from-and-to-the-hurting-before-mothers-day/.

4. Matthew Henry, *Matthew Henry's Commentary on the Bible,* accessed May 28, 2015.

5. "*Shama*," Blue Letter Bible, accessed June 22, 2015.

Chapter 4

1. Lara Williams, "Fill Us, Lord, to Overflowing" (blog), accessed December 4, 2015, http://tooverflowing.com/.

2. Herbert Lockyer, *All the Women of the Bible* (Grand Rapids, MI: Zondervan, 1988) on Bible Gateway, accessed June 11, 2015, https://www.biblegateway.com/resources/all-women-bible/Hannah.

3. Jon Bloom, "Lay Aside the Weight of Prideful Comparison," September 13, 2013, accessed June 4, 2015, http://www.desiringgod.org/articles/lay-aside-the-weight-of-prideful-comparison.

Chapter 5

1. G.K. Chesterton, "The Red Angel," *Tremendous Trifles* (New York: Dodd, Mead & Company, 1909).

2. Stacey Thacker and Brooke McGlothlin, *Hope for the Weary Mom: Let God Meet You in the Mess* (Eugene, OR: Harvest House, 2015), 74-75.

3. Matthew Henry, *Matthew Henry's Commentary on the Bible,* accessed July 7, 2015.

4. Elisabeth Elliot, *Keep a Quiet Heart* (Ann Arbor, MI: Servant Publications, 1995), 99.

5. Matthew Henry, *Matthew Henry's Commentary on the Bible*, accessed July 8, 2015.

6. François Villon, "I die of thirst beside the fountain," in *The Poems of François Villon*, trans. Galway Kinnell (New York: Houghton Mifflin, 1982), 177.

7. Matthew Henry, *Matthew Henry's Commentary on the Bible,* accessed July 8, 2015.

8. Nancy Leigh DeMoss, *Lies Women Believe and the Truth That Sets Them Free* (Chicago, IL: Moody Press, 2001), 33.

Chapter 6

1. C.S. Lewis, *The Problem of Pain* (San Francisco: HarperOne, 2009), 91.

2. Matthew Henry, *Matthew Henry's Commentary on the Bible*, accessed October 9, 2015.

3. John Piper, *A Sweet and Bitter Providence: Sex, Race, and the Sovereignty of God* (Wheaton, IL: Crossway Books, 2009).

4. Ibid.

5. Ibid.

6. "Bethlehem," Blue Letter Bible, accessed July 21, 2015.

7. Erin French, interviewed on *The Chew*, ABC, June 17, 2015.

8. Charles Spurgeon, "Morning—July 1," *Morning and Evening* (New Kensington, PA: Whitaker House, 2001), July 1.

Chapter 7

1. "Cry," Blue Letter Bible, accessed July 29, 2015.

2. Elisabeth Elliot, *Keep a Quiet Heart* (Ann Arbor, MI: Servant Publications, 1995), 45.

3. Watchman Nee, *Sit, Walk, Stand* (Carol Stream, IL: Tyndale House Publishers, 1977), 11.

4. Kelly Minter, *Ruth: Loss, Love, and Legacy* (Nashville, TN: Lifeway, 2009), 103.

Chapter 8

1. Ed Bez, "Ancient Watchtowers," *Under the Olive Tree* (blog), August 21, 2011, http://www.undertheot.com/blog/ancient-watchtowers.

2. Alan Boyle, "Dried Up Grass Reveals the Secret of Stonehenge's Circle," September 2, 2014, http://www.nbcnews.com/science/science-news/dried -grass-reveals-secret-stonehenges-circle-n194256.

3. A.W. Tozer, *The Pursuit of God* (Camp Hill, PA: Christian Publications, Inc., 1982), 73.

4. Ibid., 76.

5. Ibid., 82.

6. Nancy Leigh DeMoss, "Cultivating Intimacy with Christ," Revive Our Hearts Radio, June 16, 2014, https://www.reviveourhearts.com/radio/ revive-our-hearts/cultivating-intimacy-christ-1/.

7. Mark Buchanan, *The Rest of God* (Nashville, TN: Thomas Nelson, 2006), 125.

Chapter 9

1. "*Ba'ar,*" Blue Letter Bible, accessed August 15, 2015.

2. Don Fortner, "Watch, Write, Wait" (sermon), November 7, 2010, accessed November 23, 2015, http://www.donfortner.com/sermon_notes/35_habak kuk-series/hab%2012%2002v02-04%20Watch,%20Write,%20Wait,%20 Believe.htm.

3. Julie Cameron, *The Right to Write: An Invitation and Initiation into the Writing Life* (New York: Tarcher/Putnam, 1998), xvi.

4. Maria Konnikova, "What's Lost as Handwriting Fades," *The New York Times*, June 2, 2014, http://www.nytimes.com/2014/06/03/science/whats-lost-as -handwriting-fades.html.

5. Ibid.

6. David Mathis, "Journal as a Pathway to Joy," *Desiring God* (blog), July 30, 2014, http://www.desiringgod.org/articles/journal-as-a-pathway-to-joy.

7. Ibid.

Chapter 10

1. Warren Wiersbe, *The Wiersbe Bible Commentary: Old Testament* (Colorado Springs, CO: David C. Cook, 2007), 1479.

2. Matthew Henry, *Matthew Henry's Commentary on the Bible*, accessed August 24, 2015.

3. Karla M. Kincannon, "Silence Is Golden," *Ministry Matters* (blog), August 20, 2011, http://www.ministrymatters.com/all/entry/633/silence-is-golden.

4. Matthew Henry, *Matthew Henry's Commentary on the Bible*, accessed August 24, 2015.

5. Ann Voskamp, *Unwrapping the Greatest Gift* (Carol Stream, IL: Tyndale, 2014), 115.

6. "Habakkuk Commentary—Chapter 3," *Precept Austin*, September 10, 2012, https://preceptaustin.wordpress.com/2012/09/10/habakkuk-3-commentary/.

7. A.W. Tozer, *Worship: The Missing Jewel* (Camp Hill, PA: Christian Publications, Inc., 1992), 21.

8. Martha Munizzi, First Baptist Orlando EQ Workshop, July 18, 2015.

9. Arthur Bennett, ed., *The Valley of Vision: A Collection of Puritan Prayers and Devotions* (Carlisle, PA: The Banner of Truth Trust, 1975).

Chapter 11

1. Matthew Henry, *Matthew Henry's Commentary on the Bible*, accessed September 1, 2015.

2. Steven J. Cole, "The Throne of Grace (Hebrews 4:14-16)" at Bible.org, accessed September 1, 2015, https://bible.org/seriespage/lesson-14-throne-grace-hebrews-414-16.

3. David Weigel, "Crowds Flock to Georgia to Pay Tribute to Cancer-Stricken Jimmy Carter," *The Washington Post*, August 30, 2015, http://www.washingtonpost.com/politics/crowds-flock-to-georgia-to-pay-tribute-to-cancer-stricken-jimmy-carter/2015/08/30/ef3783c6-4f3f-11e5-933e-7d06c647a395_story.html.

4. Matthew Henry, *Matthew Henry's Commentary on the Bible*, accessed September 3, 2015.

5. "Mercy," Blue Letter Bible, accessed September 3, 2015.

6. "Consumed," Blue Letter Bible, accessed September 4, 2015.

7. Thacker and McGlothlin, *Hope for the Weary Mom*, 62.

8. Cole, "The Throne of Grace."

9. Raechel Myers, "The Washing of Regeneration," She Reads Truth (blog), June 9, 2014, http://shereadstruth.com/2014/06/09/washing-regeneration/.

10. Brennan Manning, *Abba's Child: Expanded Edition* (Colorado Springs, CO: NavPress, 2002), 29.

11. You can see some of Lori's jewelry at facebook.com/Kory-Lane-Designs -168685443337905.

12. John Stocker, "Thy Mercy, My God, Is the Theme of My Song," *The Hartford Selection of Hymns* (1799), hymnary.org, accessed September 7, 2015, http://www.hymnary.org/text/thy_mercy_my_god_is_the_theme_of_my_song.

Afterword

1. These three websites—all accessed on December 5, 2015—were valuable resources for the discussion of Capernaum:

http://www.abarim-publications.com/Meaning/Capernaum.html
http://www.biblewalks.com/Sites/capernaum.html
http://www.waynestiles.com/capernaum-jesus-slept-here-and-why/

2. This phrase is from the editorial introduction to Isaiah 9 in The Voice.

Do you ever feel like you're fresh out of amazing? Daily pouring yourself out for your family, you're tired, overwhelmed, and have nothing left to give. *Hope for the Weary Mom* is an honest look at where you find yourself living. In their new book, bloggers Stacey Thacker and Brooke McGlothlin (creators of the online communities *Mothers of Daughters* and *The MOB Society*) lead you to the God who meets you in your mess and show you that you don't walk through life alone. You will...

- invite God into your mess
- reconnect with His heart for you
- experience the peace and freedom of walking with Him

It's easy to forget that God knows you by name when you're numb with the daily grind. Join Stacey and Brooke and begin the journey from weariness to hope.

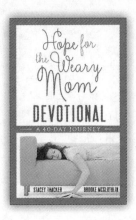

From the authors of *Hope for the Weary Mom* comes a new 40-day devotional.

Jesus promises rest to those who seek Him. But how can a weary mom find rest in Jesus when she doesn't know Him? How can she build her life on the truth of His Word when she doesn't know it? *Hope for the Weary Mom Devotional* offers 40 truths every mom needs to know in a devotional format—easy for a busy mom to fit in her life. Discover how to

- live dependently upon Jesus as his Word becomes more rooted in your heart.
- move from weariness to hope in your God-given role as mom.
- focus on who God is and how He moves and works in your life.

Each devotion includes a prayer, Scripture, and questions for reflection. You'll be moved to deeper truth and be left with a hunger for more of God's Word.

Connect with Stacey Thacker!

 facebook.com/29LincolnAvenue

 @staceythacker

 @staceythacker

And be sure to visit StaceyThacker.com
for the latest news, blog posts, and more!

Stacey Thacker is wife to Mike and the mother of four vibrant girls. She is a writer and speaker who loves God's Word, preferably with a good cup of coffee. Her passion is to connect with women and encourage them in their walks with God. Stacey is the founder of *Mothers of Daughters*, a popular blog for modern moms wanting to raise girls according to timeless truth and vintage values.

To learn more about books by Stacey Thacker
or to read sample chapters, visit our website:
www.harvesthousepublishers.com